MW00909058

THE INVISIBLE CHILD

Healing the Damage
Of
Childhood Sexual Abuse

The Invisible Child:
Healing The Damage
Of
Childhood Sexual Abuse

Published by

Heart Whispers
~~**1220 Airline, Suite 130 #196-G**~~ *PO Bx 81311*
Corpus Christi, TX ~~**78412**~~ *78468*

First Edition: January 1999

ISBN: 0-9668888-0-4

Cover Art
by
Lyn Price

Printed in the USA by

3212 East Highway 30 • Kearney, NE 68847 • 1-800-650-7888

DEDICATION

To Julia Gail
and
all other invisible children –
may your broken wings heal gently

ACKNOWLEDGMENTS

There are so many wonderful people that were a part of my healing to whom I would like to say "thank you," although these two simple words hardly seem adequate enough to convey the depth of gratitude that I truly feel. I can only trust, then, that each individual will look inside their hearts and know how much I appreciate the support, encouragement and hope they provided on those days when I most needed to feel safe until I could find my way through the darkness of my pain to celebrate passage into the light of new life. This book would never have been written at all without their patient nurturing, forgiving hearts, and gentle guidance.

Much love is given to my spiritual parents, Gerald and Phyllis Lee, Maudie Thrush and Arline Logue (both of whom now dance with the angels in Heaven), Moriah Howland, Sami Wolf, Sherri and Craig Lee, Brenda Bowden, Richard S. Orton., Betty Glasson, Wanda Box, Peggy Hattersly, Sidney Balster, Bea Ross, Sandra Coughlin, Susan Liberto, Schuyler Schmidt, Martha Adams, Allen and Melissa Cook, Paula Barstad, Pam Cross, Wes Harris, Fran Thompson, and Dr. Marvarene Oliver. Also, special "thanks" to my awesome Net friends Maximillian Zayas, Jo Taylor, Bridgette Heath, Rajat Mathur, Sarah Mackenstein, David H. James, Jr. and Daniel Strayhorn for the friendship, laughter, and learning they brought to the final stages of this book. Lyn Price taught by example how to be a better friend both to myself and others. Hers is a magical, sensitive soul, and I love her deeply as a precious friend. Peggy Gillis bestowed upon my path her unique gift of spiritual introspection and unconditional acceptance. She continues to be a treasured, loving (and smart!) friend and source of new growth for me. Debrah Magee, my first counselor, encouraged me to put all my thoughts and feelings into words. As I grew, she taught me that sharing my work could help heal others, and for this truth I am eternally grateful. Faye O'Neal gave countless hours to making manuscript corrections, in addition to providing kaleidoscopes and laughter when I got frustrated and seriously questioned whether or not I could finish all the work that had to be done. She is an awesome inspiration to my continuing journey. Veronica S. Gutierrez was patient, professional and did a magnificent job of manuscript preparation. I am thankful to Jo Ann Valerio, Janet and Charlie Zepeda, Don and Terri Stone, and Tom Hawkins for their individual contributions to this project. I am most thankful to God, for He was with me as a child and throughout my years as a lonely, frightened adult in despair. My life was spared countless times, and I am humbly grateful for this opportunity to use this gift of poetic expression to now serve others according to His purpose for my life.

You are my family
and
I love you with all that I am.

CONTENTS

AUTHOR'S NOTE

PART I
POETRY WRITTEN BEFORE I REMEMBERED

PART II
. . . AND THE VEIL OF LOST TIME LIFTED

PART III
HEALING TRANSFORMATION

AUTHOR'S NOTE

I am a healing survivor of childhood sexual abuse
and incest.

It is my desire to be a voice for other survivors and
to put forth my truth so that perhaps one of you who reads
this book will come to know, as I have, that you are not
alone on your journey to healing. It is not an easy journey,
and no one can make it for you, but the rewards you will
find as you walk toward recovery are ones that make every
tear you cry, every emotion you discover, and every truth
you face well worth the effort and time you expend. Peace
and serenity, feelings you may never have known in your
lifetime or may have doubted you deserved to experience,
are waiting for you. You will find the truth of your life, but
more importantly, you will finally know who you are and
not be dependent on someone else's choices for your
identity.

The poetry that I share within the pages of "The
Invisible Child" fall into three periods of time:

Part 1, "Poetry Written Before I Remembered,"
consists of poetry written between 1985 and September 30,
1993. They are reflective of the depression, the years of
drug addiction, and the haunting that I felt while not
knowing why inner-darkness was such an integral part of
my life.

Part 2 of my book, " ... And The Veil Of Lost Time
Lifted," consists of poetry written during my initial stages
of remembering the details of incest with which I had never
before dealt. Although I was not in any type of therapy

when these memories were "triggered" on October 11, 1993, writing the details of what I remembered, as well as keeping a journal of my feelings, helped me sort through the confusion and often mind-numbing emotional pain I experienced when my biological family made it clear that no validation or belief of my memories would be forthcoming. I chose to detach myself from my family in December 1993 so that I could seek therapy and find my own answers. This was a personal decision, based on the obvious and fragmented structure of my own family's dysfunctional attitudes.

I feel compelled to pause here and clarify that I do not in any way mean to convey to my readers that detachment from one's family is necessarily the only option available to survivors when dealing with the trauma of remembering abuse and incest. Occasionally, disclosure of abuse can be a foundation on which a broken family can begin to heal. For me, however, it became clear after speaking with family members that detachment was the appropriate option for me if I were ever to know the entirety of my truth based on my own memories and life-experiences. Otherwise, I would stay prisoner to the denial of my family and chaos that followed when disclosure of the abuse and incest was confronted.

Part 3 of this book, "Healing Transformation," contains poetry written during the stage of my healing when I finally began to experience spans of time that were free of the emotional pain of remembering. As I continued to work through my issues in therapy and through my writing, I began to have days, and eventually weeks and months, filled with the discovery of positive attitudes and healthy choices. During this time, too, I remembered specific events from my childhood that were fun and normal. These memories created a welcome break from the daily darkness I had experienced while dealing with my own specific memories of abuse, and served as affirmation that I was on the right path. This time was rewarding as I persevered through the raw horror of remembering the incest and the many difficult choices I had made toward the rebirth of my own humanity.

To my readers who are survivors, this book is not intended to be offered as advice, nor do I wish it to be used in lieu of licensed therapy should your particular situation warrant that. Should you choose therapy, try to keep an open mind but be prepared to work more diligently toward your recovery than you have ever worked toward anything in your life. Reading certain parts of my story may feel familiar and be upsetting to you. Perhaps what I have written can be used by you to show your therapist in a way that is safe for you what issues you need to address at a pace *you* are comfortable with. If at any time you feel overwhelmed by the emotions you encounter, please stop reading until you are in a safe place to speak with a therapist and work through your emotions together. My prayer is that my willingness to share my story will help you in some small way as you seek to find your individual answers and serve to inspire you to use what you learn on your journey to help others.

To my readers who are non-survivors, I trust that "The Invisible Child" will bring enlightenment to your life and leave you with awareness of the scope of the living nightmare that millions of victims of childhood sexual abuse and incest are forced to endure every day. The totality of devastation to the spirit and life that such abuse can cause and the difficult road survivors must travel in order to fully recover from the choices that others have made against them may be frightening to confront if you have never experienced it personally. I believe, however, that we can learn from one another and we can help each other grow by sharing our feelings openly and honestly. Only then can we acknowledge and help heal the humanity of those who remain buried as nameless, faceless corpses in a complacent society's statistical graveyard - America's sexually abused children.

God's peace be with you.

Many years ago, I asked my mother, "What was I like when I was a little girl? Was I cute? Did I have friends? Did I play? Was I shy or outgoing?" Mother was quiet for a few moments before answering.

"You were a bad child, Judy," she said. "You told lies all the time, stole things from school, and I don't know why you were so desperate for attention. When you were just a little girl of five or six, I would be working around the house and realize I hadn't seen you for awhile. I'd find you hiding in a corner somewhere or in one of the closet storage spaces. Sometimes you'd be sitting under one of the tables. You weren't playing. You were just sitting there quietly in the dark. Your dad and I had five of you kids, and I swear, people thought we only had four. You were so quiet and withdrawn as a child; it was like you were invisible. Sitting in the dark, invisible."

She was vocalizing the feeling that had saturated every aspect of my life for as far back as I could remember.

Bad. In the dark. Invisible.

And so,
life went on . . .

PART I

POETRY WRITTEN
BEFORE I REMEMBERED

NO TIME

little girl
living in the shadows
little girl
playing in the night
little girl
hiding in the darkness
little girl
faded is your light

  lonely girl
  watching other children
  lonely girl
  longing to take part
  lonely girl
  aching to be someone
  lonely girl
  you break your mother's heart

  frightened girl
  looking out the window
  frightened girl
  growing way too fast
  frightened girl
  locked tight within your prison
  frightened girl
  trapped sinking in your past

  woman-child
  gone are all your chances
  woman-child
  Fate has claimed its prize
  woman-child
  there will be no tomorrow
  woman-child
  Death sleeps within your eyes

3

FANTASY

sometimes I fantasize
that I am like
all the other people
I come in contact with every day
I fantasize
about what it might feel like
waking up just one day
and
having a purpose
some small reason to be glad
that I am alive
I wonder what it would be like
to greet the sunlight
with open arms
instead of dread and foreboding

when the sun is gone
and
evening shadows
fall upon my face
only then can I be myself
and look inside
at the unspoken truths
that rest in my heart

in the darkness
I am safe
seems like
it has always been that way

in the darkness
I can dream
pretend
I am someone else

in the darkness
I can escape reality
hide from the morning light
that threatens to expose me

I have lived in the darkness
I have coped with the light
I have never had a choice
but to survive

STIFLE IT

don't let anyone
inside your heart –
they might know you

don't let anyone
know you –
they might care

don't let anyone
care for you –
they might hurt you

don't let anyone hurt you –
you have been there
too many times before

FEELINGS

I laugh
      and
it feels foreign to me
           laughter isn't something
           I've had a lot of time for
             in my life

I cry
      and
it feels as if
a dam will burst
somewhere inside me
           tears frighten me
          so I
           dry them
             and deny that there is pain

I smile
      and
say what I think
everyone else wants to hear
           I'm sure
           that is what
           they expect anyway

                    I don't know anything about feelings
years ago
  I put them all away
in an invisible box
and
tucked them away
safely to sleep inside
                              the parents
                              and
                              others in my life
                              told me what I
                              should or shouldn't feel
      for once
  I guess I obeyed
        because
      I have nothing left
        except for what
      they think I need
          to get by
              and
          this is okay
        because I have accepted
            that my life
          is never going to be
            any different.

PLEASE WAIT

please wait for me
I am on a long journey
trying to find out just who I am

please don't hurry me
I need your patience
and acceptance
to find my own way

please wait for me
and though
I may test your limits sometimes
it is only
because
I have walked a lonely road
all of my life
and
I want to make sure
the path that I choose
is the right one for me

please wait for me
and don't give up

I am begging you
don't forget
that I exist

HEROES

I used to believe in heroes

in my childhood innocence
I believed that the day would come
when
my champion would cease to be fantasy
and become reality

in my world there would be
no sadness
no hurting
no disappointment in others
every day
would be an exhilarating temptation
for my imagination

though the years passed
and
my hero never came
I grew into womanhood despite its non-existence

even now that I am grown sometimes
I find myself searching for that lost hero
someone
tangible to grasp hold of
someone
to cling to in the night
a place to journey
not shrouded in fear

yet I
know I must make my own way
I
know I must find strength within myself

I
must learn if there is life within me
instead of existing with a truth
which frightens me each step of the way

my hero
is a vanishing dream

TRUST

what is trust?

is it something I was born with
and then
somebody stole it from me
when I was too young
to know how to fight to keep it?

have I ever experienced
this bewildering emotion called trust?

how can I trust
when all my choices have been made for me?
how can I trust
when my future has been decided
by what has taken place in my past?
how can I trust
when my identity was stolen from me
by someone or something
that I can't remember?

I alone
bear the scars of my past
so how can you or anyone else
expect me to trust you
with knowledge of my innermost secrets
when I can't even feel safe enough
to search for the truth of those secrets myself?

if I trust someone
allow *anyone* to be close enough
to my emotions
how can I be sure
that it won't be a decision
I pay for with my sanity?

the risk is too much for me

I can't take it

WHO WILL LOVE ME?

who will love me
>   with my shattered dreams
>>   my anguished soul
>>   and
>>   my aching heart?

who will love me
>   with my aged mind
>>   my secret scars
>>   and
>>   my barren fear?

who will love me
>   with my pseudo smile
>>   my silent tears
>>   and
>>   my tortured rage?

there is none who will love me
>   because
>>   I'm *dead* inside.

FIVE WORDS I'LL NEVER HEAR

ALL   I   NEED   TO   BECOME   REAL
IS
FOR
JUST
ONE
PERSON
TO
REACH FOR MY HAND
TOUCH
MY
TIRED
SKIN
CONNECT   WITH   MY   EYES
AND
SAY
THE
WORDS
NOBODY
EVER
LOVED
ME
ENOUGH
TO
SAY

"I'M SORRY FOR YOUR PAIN"

what is wrong with me
that nobody can love me?

16

VAPOR

I do not know why I exist

a sea of grief crashes against my soul
but I do not know why I grieve

a primal child-like scream escapes my lips
but there is no sound to my pain

a clinched fist of rage squeezes me breathless
but I do not know why I am angry

I can express nothing
because I do not feel

I consider calling my family
the strangers whose blood is
part of my existence
but they don't want to hear the truth
just happy lies
or cheerful letters that say
"everything is fine"
so I continue
my familiar way of coping
rather than risk having no family at all

I consider calling a friend
but no name comes to mind
there are those who say they care
but yet have never noticed
there is no life within me
I wonder
what they would say
if they knew that I breathe
but think about release in dying
when the dope is gone
and I have nothing to give them
the telephone is silent
the house is empty
then
pay-day comes around again
and they know
I'll spend every penny I have
I'd rather be poor
than face the reality that
none of them care at all

I know what the face of abandonment looks like
I've been looking at it all of my life
that face is there
stoned and staring
whenever I have something to offer
and I hear
"we are so happy to see you again!"

I consider talking to God
but God doesn't exist
for people like me
the church would argue
"God lives within us all"
but when I look inside
there is black emptiness
and I don't see God
stopping *my* pain . . .
> God is only there
> for those who
> sit in the front row
> of a church
> sing the loudest
> nod their head
> and whisper "Amen"

> I've been around them since I was a kid
> and not one of them noticed
> that I died a long time ago

I am a vapor
hovering ever so slightly above the ground
and today I am afraid
because
it is a very windy day

- September 30, 1993

PART II

... AND
THE VEIL OF LOST TIME
LIFTED

THE INVISIBLE CHILD

little girl with vacant eyes
no one hears her anguished cries
face upturned to Heaven above
she only wants her mother's love

        mother is busy – so much to do
        baby sister wants attention, too
        oh! little girl, where went your dreams?
        she plays alone in concrete streams

find a corner in the night
no one knows to soothe her fright
mother is tired and needs her sleep
silent pain will no tears weep

survival says that she must deal
with voiceless wounds that do not heal
the veil of time is floating past
at 6 years old, she is fading fast

alone at night she lies awake
oh! dread the nightmare that her peace does take!
guilt and shame that do not end
she begs, "dear Jesus, angels send!"

how can it be that none did see
a child who grew with no memories?
oh! mourn her loss of time and youth!
asleep is her deep-buried truth!

when walking down a hurried street
how oft we judge those that we meet
by length of hair or who holds their hand
we do not stop to understand
we each deserve truth reconciled

what will open your eyes to
the invisible child?

REMEMBERING

the wall of my inner-prison is broken down
brick after brick gives way
and
all I can see
is
devastation and loss

my life lies before me
the ruins of betrayal
a maddening jumble of images
where before there have only been
lost spans of time

blank spaces
are filled in
there is
a
shift in vision
and
I view my life clearly
for the first time

I don't want to know this

I didn't believe in God
but
yelled at the heavens
"I need answers!"
and
now it feels like
I am tumbling
over the edge of sanity
spiraling into
that which
I have not remembered
but
now must face

the fear I feel consumes
every fiber of my body
I try to sleep
hoping I will wake up
and
not have to
look at it anymore
but
sleep isn't my friend
never has been
and
when I close my eyes
images of touching and pain
flash across my tired mind

this makes no sense . . .

I feel
as if someone has
flipped a switch inside me
and
I alone am left
to feel the touches
and
see the faces
of those who hurt me
I can smell their sweat
and
hear their lies as they ruin me
over and over and over again

why doesn't someone make it stop?

what is happening to me?

WHERE AM I?

I see
a light outside the window
a green tie with yellow stripes
light red eyebrows
teeth (they're so straight!)
a black camera box
an index file under a car seat
my pajamas on the floor
white curtains pulled shut
and
an open suitcase on the dresser

I smell
Old Spice cologne
sweaty armpits
beer on warm breath
a greasy hot dog
cigarettes in an ashtray
salt
mint toothpaste
Pine-sol
and
vomit and urine

I hear
somebody laughing
grunting
whispering (shh! I won't hurt you)
the radio playing "Little Red Riding Hood"
traffic outside on the street
snoring
someone whimpering
gagging noises
and
a toilet flushing

I feel
a callused hand stroking my forehead
a hand on my tummy
sticky stuff in my hand
something hard on my thigh
prickles on my neck
I can't breathe!
someone pinching me
I can't breathe!
vomit coming up
and
I think it's my fault

where am I?
where is my mother?

everything is mixed together
but
it doesn't matter
because
I know how to disappear.

BLANK

I remember

           cartoons on Saturday mornings
          Baskin Robbins on Sunday afternoons
        church services on Wednesday evenings

and

   a nightmare that blanketed my childhood nights

I remember

           gold sparkles on a den ceiling
          heat lamps on a bathroom ceiling
       brown rafters across a living room ceiling

and

   white plaster bumpy things on a bedroom ceiling

I remember

           a motel room number – 117
         a motel bedspread – brown with big flowers
      motel curtains – white, dirty around the edges

and

   a motel shower stall, water running

                              I dig around in my memory
                    searching . . .
          searching . . .
                                        searching . . .
I try to remember
        mother smiling
          father smiling
            sisters or brother smiling
                              I try to remember
                              (people)
                              but
                              my memory is
              blank.

37

MOLESTED!

I am caught up
in
a cyclone
of memories
coming out
from the recesses
of my mind
it feels like
some kind of
crazy
Mental Slide Show

it is no use
trying to sleep
I've been awake
for days
I lie down
exhausted
from the crying
then I snap awake
back to the world
where I must function

I sit
eyes closed
with my knees
pulled close to my chest
my head down
and I am
remembering . . .

in the course of my day
I see a
convenience store clerk
postman
gas station attendant
people
I do not know
but
I feel different than I did
when I didn't have to remember

now
when anyone looks at me
I wonder
if they see
(can they see?)
the invisible brand on my forehead
opening my past for all to view
you know the brand I'm talking about
it screams
"I WAS MOLESTED!"

FEAR

what if

I quit denying what I know happened
look at the truth no matter how much it hurts
somehow learn to feel emotions
and
when all the layers of abuse are stripped away
there is
nothing left
to my
identity?

what if

I remember every little detail
confront who I am
and beneath all the destruction
that has been my life
I really am
nobody
like I've been told
all of these years?

what if
I never existed
at all?

I have never been so afraid.

RUINS

I am crushed
      suffocated
                  beneath the weight
                      of
                30 plus years gone
                    void
                  of emotion
I feel
      empty
            and
violated
               nothing makes any sense
                  and
              what I am remembering
                confuses me

if I believe
the images
that flash

across my tired mind

then
I will have to accept
that everything
I have ever known
is a lie
designed by
my father
and my family
to keep me
from ever knowing
the truth
of my life

pieces of me are dead
        and
                no amount of frantic searching
                for a pulse to prove they ever
                existed at all will resurrect them

oh God
        how could he hurt me?
        what did I do to make
        my father hurt me?

                can somebody please tell me
            how did I survive?

THE FAMILY DUMP

the garbage of my father's abuse
the trash of my mother's convenient blindness
the scum of my brother's insanity
the stench of my sister's ignorance
their intolerance
their denial of the truth
their need to *blame* me
for being a trusting child
has all been dumped into my lap
and they expect me to keep
living with it
eating with it
and
sleeping with it

Family wants me to apologize
                    and I won't
they want me to change the truth
                    and I won't
      but most incredible of all
            Family stands like scavenging vultures
                  waiting for me to
                  screw up again
            so they can clap their hands
                  in delight
                  and say,
                  "See,
            we told you that
            you are a *failure*"

so today
I started
picking at the edges of wounds
that never healed
screamed in pain
but decided to rip them all open anyway
let them hemorrhage
if that's what they need to do
squeeze out the pus
of lies and family secrets
and
finally figured out
I don't have to wear the label
"Family Dumping Ground"
anymore

I gather up all the raw sewage
of my past
and throw it
right back into the face of my father
where it belonged
the minute he decided
to lay his filthy hands on me
and
I no longer accept his damage.

KEEPER OF SECRETS

my mother
is
and
always has been
a
Keeper Of Secrets.

all these years
I have been afraid of telling her
the truth of my life
just how messed up things really were
for fear of being yet
another disappointment to her
time after time
I needed her comfort
but she didn't care how I felt
she tolerated me
and
probably sighed with relief
when I would leave once more

I tell my mother now
what I am remembering
tell her I am afraid she will hate me
and she says
"I will believe you
no matter what you say
because
I am your mother"

then she realizes
she's going to have to look at the truth
she starts crying
and says
"what about me?"

yeah
what about *her* indeed . . .

I tell her
I remember lying in my bed
waiting for her to rescue me
from my father's hands
a dark corner in a motel room
trying to cope with the terror
I remember thinking
"mommy will come get me"
but she never
walked through the door

I've heard for years
what a bad kid I was
listened to her tell me
a thousand times
what she wanted me to know
she was safe
knowing I didn't remember
I *asked* her
and
what I got were
select pieces of
convenient memories
of my childhood
so it was always
somehow my fault
for causing
her pain

mother tells me
I don't know what
she went through
because of my father
and she's right
because she never told me
she
just keeps right on playing
the role of
Keeper Of Secrets
and making me feel like shit
so no finger will point
in her direction

I think back
over the years
to her
averted eyes
and cautious manipulation
away from the questions
I asked her
about the years
I couldn't remember

I spent the entirety of my life
waiting for her to
tell me she was glad I was born
I
distanced myself in miles and emotions
feeling
I could never be good enough
for her to love me
I
got used to things
being so messed up
and
accepting that
everything that went wrong
was because I was too stupid to learn
and
deserved nothing better
than to cope with and hide
the pain

now
I have to face the memories
and
I alone
feel the betrayal
of having no choice
but to
confront the truth
that
my mother has known all along
my father touched me
and
to save *her* own ass
from being inconvenienced
and
to keep from being left alone
with five kids to raise
she kept his secret
setting me up
time after time
to be alone with him

I love my mother
and
would rather be dead
than accept
that
she never wanted me to know
the whole truth
but
I hate her
with the pain
and
with the fury
of
the thousands of lost nights
that are gone forever . . .

she said
I was nothing
she said
I was a bad little girl
and
I think
my mother
hated me.

AT THE EDGE

I am standing at the edge
  of the only world I know
    balancing precariously
      daring myself to look inward
          and
        glancing furtively from side to side
          at the sea of faces
        familiar yet foreign to me
hoping
     needing
       someone
  to save me from myself
      and
  provide to me the key
    to unlock the shadow chains
     that bind me
         hand and foot
         body and soul
           to a past
     that I can only vaguely remember
       but am certain
      that I cannot erase

emotions elude me
        hazy half-memories confuse me
     and
I am exhausted
   from crippled attempts
      to keep my sanity intact
             on this
            crumbling precipice
       of
time-worn
    e
   x
     i
      s
       t
        e
         n
          c
           e

somewhere within me
slumbers a strange child
I think I once knew
I can sense her outstretched arms
reaching for me to acknowledge her
but instead
my fear consumes me
and I
deny her identity
and
force her to retreat
out of some belated
and misguided
perception of obligation
to keep her safely hidden

but
to speak her name
feels as though
it might be
the ultimate betrayal
of all she never got to be

where are my tears?
        where is my outrage
        at the pain she suffered?
                        why can't I feel anymore?
        what evil deeds did I commit
        so that *she* endured such sorrow?

            I ask myself these questions

                        but

            there are no answers

I am standing at the edge
   of the only world I know
      balancing precariously
         as I feel
            the storms of change
              begin to rage
            more fiercely than ever before
                      and
                unable to steady my feet
                 I tumble over the edge
                  into the darkness

when I dare breathe again
        I glance inward once more
and
        begin to weep with grief-stricken shame
            at the somber, staring face
          and
              the unexpressed hurting
                of a dying child . . .

I must be punished for what I have done to her.

alone she cried

dear god at birth i had your light
to play and dream as was my right
then my daddy stole your light away
he said you don't hear bad girls pray

i try real hard to understand why
i must live with daddy's lie
my daddy says he loves me best
but when night comes i cannot rest

my daddy hurts me, god, please hear
i dare not shed a single tear
please, god, forgive me i know i'm bad
i'm sorry i make my mommy sad

dear god, why have you turned away?
is there something i can do or say
to make you love me once again
and stop my daddy's hands of sin?

i'm very tired and need to sleep
i feel so sad and ache so deep
it's hard to say "thy will be done"
when pain is what i know will come

dear god, please help my eyes to see
that others hurt, they're just like me
my daddy's touch has left me cold
dear god, i'm only 5 years old

PHOTOGRAPHS

at 1 year old I was adorable
at 2 years old I was shy
at 3 years old I was sensitive
                              and
at 4 years old my eyes began to plead . . .
          at 5 years old I was vulnerable
          at 6 years old I was aging
          at 7 years old I was searching
          at 8 years old I was coping
          at 9 years old I was numb
          at 10 years old I was vacant
                              and
at 11 years old
          7 years of molestation were taking their toll . . .
at 12 years old I was raped
at 13 years old I was pregnant
at 14 years old I was addicted
at 15 years old I was running
at 16 years old I was desperate
at 17 years old I was coping
                              and
at 18 years old
          I no longer cared . . .

nobody noticed

                                        nobody cared
                         the camera captured it all
black and white   color   posed and natural

64

I confront the people
I called
Family
scream my anger
ask them
"how could you not see?:

they hang on to their
thin, unraveling lifeline
of denial
and scream back their answer
"quit telling lies about your father!"

moving on through the album . . .

there I am
    as little Judy
        sitting on daddy's lap
          his "special favorite" (yeah, right)
            and the bastard
              has his hand on my leg
there I am
    as teen-age Judy
        sitting on the floor with a puppy
              and
          pressed close behind
            way too near
              is my daughter-molesting father
                with a smile on his face
there I am
    as different-ages Judy
        standing in family photographs
          among people I do not know
            and there is
                daddy standing next to Judy
              Daddy Standing Next To Judy
            daddy standing next to Judy
              and
        I have all the proof
        I am ever going to need.

CODE OF SILENCE

Family
doesn't want to talk about
how as a little girl of six
I knew how to
paralyze my legs
("PSYCHOLOGICALLY INDUCED –
NO MEDICAL CAUSE KNOWN")
to get out
of going on another business trip
with my father
or
how I gave away all of my toys
so
I would have friends
or
how I played alone in the dark
until mother noticed she hadn't
seen me for a while
and came looking for me
or
how I woke up crying
night after night
from the same nightmare
or
how I didn't tell when
the neighbor boy touched me
the same way my father did

Family
doesn't want to talk about
how I rose up early every morning
before school to sort through
my dresses no matter how much
snow was on the ground
looking for a one-piece jumper
to make it hard for the boys
at school to pinch my breasts
or
how many times I took off riding on our horse
and stayed gone for hours at a time in a
futile attempt to get away from
brother's hands in my pants
or
when I grew to be a teen-ager, I was pregnant
at 13 years old (but, of course,
that didn't happen, either) and miscarried
waiting for three months
until mother finally noticed
I was bleeding to the point of almost
needing a transfusion but put off
taking me to a doctor until after
she and father got home from their
cruise . . .

Family
won't talk about those things
because
the
CODE OF SILENCE
is strictly enforced
and
in their minds
if they do not talk about something
then
it does not exist!

decades passed
before
the memories came forward
to be dealt with
and
when confronted with the truth
Family
suddenly decides
maybe
they have a few things
to talk about
after all . . .

Family
rushes forward
to tell me
how curious and knowledgeable
I was about sex
as a very young child
(but not to ask who taught me, of course)
and
how I 'chose' to be
promiscuous
and
drug-addicted
by age 13
and
how a suicide attempt
was a sick way to 'get attention'
how I ran away from home
dozens of times
hurting poor suffering mother
who just
had no idea at all
why her child
had always been so *bad*

Family
has no problem remembering
my marriage to a man
who slammed my head into a wall
("what did you do to provoke him?"
loving mother asks)
how I sought the comfort of women
("always the *whore*!"
screams religious freak sister)
and
it sure is easy
to make it all
my fault
and
to complain
about the
hurt and inconvenience
I have been to
their lives

it is always about *them*

it is always about *their* feelings

not once
do they ask about *me*
not once do they ask
how *I* felt
but
that is one of many ways
a
FAMILY CODE OF SILENCE
is kept sacred

Family
hurries to blame
but does not want to know
the entire truth of my life
because
no matter what the cost
the
CODE OF SILENCE
must be kept
intact
so they won't have
to deal with the fact
that daddy started it all a long time ago
they will never acknowledge
that everything they write or scream about
but never ask me about
is
a textbook description of
a sexually abused child
when I say "here is the information"
suddenly I'm *crazy,* too

I don't need the
chaos
and
I don't need the
crap
because
I have decided
(oh yes indeed)
that whether or not
Family
wants to deal with this
I'm going to
keep asking questions
and
if I need to
tell every detail of my life
strip away all the secrets
and scrape open the wounds . . .

as I see it
there is freedom in truth
and
I no longer
am willing to be prisoner
to
Family's
CODE OF SILENCE
or take the blame
for
what wasn't
and isn't my fault at all.

SOUL FLIGHT

when the memories come
    I know that pain
        won't be too far behind
                so
I tell myself
    over and over and over again
        "it doesn't matter"
                      and
        I spread wide my inside wings
        and
        I fly away.

NIGHT PASSAGE

night passage
   into familiar territory
and I am caught
        in a web of tangled feelings

slivers of hope
  break through
     the black clouds of confrontation
        I take a deep breath
          then
      without warning or apparent cause
        the scenery of my mindscape changes
        and I
            plunge back into the abyss
              of depression

sounds of breathing
echo through my head
  warm air whispers
  against the back of my neck
    fingerless hands
    probe me intimately
        and
      I wake screaming
      because
     nobody is there

my eyes
          search for threads of truth
                              my heart
                              seeks tangible faith
                  my grief
              lies unexpressed
                              and
                      it frightens me
              to realize
                      parts of me are dead
                                          and
                          I don't know how
                                  to mourn the losses
              or
how to bury
      that which can live no more

                                  I feel
                          that I am
                                  once again
                                  a child
                  helpless
                              waiting for rescue
              but
                  nobody comes for me

I keep waiting
for the tidal wave of emotions to calm

I keep waiting
for the winds of change to shift
so
I can continue
fighting forward
and flying
on what might be
crystal wings
colored with prisms
of life-light . . .

I am tired
and
I need to rest.

PANIC

best friend
  comes around the corner
    way too fast
                just joking around
            she pins me against the wall
an image
streaks through my memory
            someone is smothering me
               I can't breathe
and
  I've been here before

I see a face

                               it's mine!

in the mirror across the hall

                                    she is

wild-eyed

      and

                  totally freaked out . . .

best friend
  apologizes profusely
    it scared her just as badly

                we sit down
                hold each other
                and
                I explain to her
                that I think
                my father is
                trying to
                    kill
                      me

best friend
  shakes me back to reality
      I start crying
        and ask her
        just how much of this
        can I take without
          going insane?

WHAT IT FEELS LIKE TO REMEMBER HIM

worms of abuse
        crawling out of my brain
                  a visual reality
      that
            I cannot erase
they multiply
      and
        swell as they devour me
                fluttering in mute rage
                then
            wailing in protest
              at their release
          from within the
             chambers of my mind
          where they have rested
            since my childhood

I hear
   collective voices in my head
     husky and moaning
    just like when I was kid
                         I sense
                collective touches on my flesh
                  hazy and fumbling
                just like when he was a man
fragmented pieces of memory
    scurrying to fit together
            shivers of fear
       racing up and down my spine
                  vaguely familiar man-scent
                  permeating my nostrils
and
      I see
           daddy's eyes
                   ash-blue eyes

I try to close my eyes

                                              I try to shut down my mind

but

                    it is no use

                                        the memories struggle

                    to keep slithering forward

groping

                          fondling

                                teasing

I remember his whisper
I remember his night
I remember the curse
he left on my skin
as he grunted his pleasure

                                    and

then disappeared inside me
never to leave again
I remember his whisper
"you're a very sexy little girl."

IF I SAY THE WORD "INCEST"

if I say the word "incest"
  connect soul to memory to mouth
    I become once again a child
        paralyzed
            shamed
  soiled
       invisible in the shadows   and
        unable to run
           from the trembling spasm
         of my father's caress

if I say the word "incest"
I see him above me
    feel his demon heat inside my body
      rotting away my young mind
        with his seed
                and
      degrading my fear
        with his mocking laughter

if I say the word "incest"
  someone is going to
                    unlock the secret
          I live hostage to
            every minute of every day
I can't tell!
              I can't tell!
                          I can't tell!
God will not forgive me
      nobody will love me
                  I don't want to be alone anymore!
        my father will be inside me again
          and I will be unable to escape
          this living death of remembering

if I say the word "incest"
connect soul to memory to mouth
someone will look closer
and reveal the disgrace
of the ancient child
that sighs wearily and
rests just beneath my eyes
someone will tell on me
someone will say this was all my fault
and then
the world will know
God, please don't hate me!
that the
bloodstains and the scars
that bathe my memory
are all that remain of what was once
an innocent baby.

NOISES

noises pounding in my headache
noises creeping in my night
noises hissing in my slumber -
a melody of fright

noises howling when I'm thinking
noises gagging when I speak
noises clouding up my vision -
an echo damp and weak

noises blinking when I whisper
noises shivering when I scream
noises sitting calm and silent -
a freeze-frame of my dreams

noises stalking in the shadows
noises fluttering in the light
noises sheltering all my secrets -
the thief of all that's right.

NIGHT DEMONS

dream tunnel
  feet running   neon snake
    end of the white line   vomiting slime
      sword straight up   under my bed covers
        soft lump of fur . . .   head raised high
                            viper's teeth smile . . .

      tiny hands
      squeezing dough
        cease my breathing
          dough oozes milk
            soul flies away . . .

. . . memory erases . . .

                              I see
                           mother
                                    standing on my doorstep
                                       our eyes meet
        father is dead
        committed suicide

                              mother laughs
                           holding his brains
                           in her outstretched hands
                              flinging them at me
                                 as punishment
                           for confronting him
                                    with my truth
"this is your fault"
   she says

                        and
                     my night demons
                     win again . . .

cloaked in darkness
   my night demons
  steal my sleep
                as I rest
           praying for peace
             they lay beside me
             waiting for my slumber

      their razor-sharp claws
       impale my dreamscape
               and
           they scream when I resist them
               and
            refuse to give them name

        then
I awaken
        to a body
                and soul
        bathed in sweat
                        my tears flow
                        and
                I feel the echo of another nightmare fading
                        retreating
                                waiting
                for surely night will fall once more

Night Demons
are patient
and
I am frightened.

GHOST HANDS

i am only 4 years old
and i am so afraid
when night comes because
when i put my head on my pink pillow
i do not know
will this be another night
that hurts
for so very many nights
i have laid alone in this dark
that is my room
i have a little bed
but it is a scary place to be
i am afraid of those hands
that reach from under my little bed
and come out of my head
those hands
they make me afraid of my dreams
those hands
they make me hide in the closet
and why doesn't mommy
or someone make those hands go away
sometimes i cry
but nobody hears me
don't i have a voice
why can nobody hear me when my screams
open up the sky outside

bad things happen in the night
bad things happen in the night
i don't like the dark
i don't like the hands
i don't like the hands
that come out of the dark
to hurt me
i don't like being scared
those hands leave behind bad things
on my skin
those hands scare me so bad
they make me cry tears
that nobody can hear
those hands
they have no arms
i am so scared
i close my eyes
and pretend those hands are gone
but they don't go away
even when i cry
and say please stop
those hands
always come back
i am just a little girl
i am so scared

i see mommy in the hall
i whisper
mommy please
make the hands go away
but she can't hear me
i know mommy sees the hands
that come from under my little bed
i say
mommy come here
i talk louder this time
but she stands there watching
and then she walks away
but the hands
the hands
they

never

    go

away
i feel them (breathing) on my face
it scares me
i dream them (monsters!) in my head
it scares me
i taste them (nasty) in my tears
it scares me
i see them (white!) in the dark
it scares me
i smell them (dirty) everywhere i go
it scares me

sometimes
when i am playing
those hands touch my back
but then i turn around
and it's just daddy
telling me
you had a bad dream last night
i want to tell him
i dreamed about the hands
under my little bed touching me
but he is smiling (where are daddy's hands?)
so i don't tell him
i don't want him to be mad again
but when he is gone
i think about the ghost hands
then at night
when i am almost asleep
i dream them again
just like daddy said i would
i taste them (i know what scared tastes like)
when i start to be afraid and cry
mommy gets so mad when i cry
she doesn't hear me
so why is she mad if she can't hear me cry

i am not real
i am a shadow
i am a tree
i am a whisper
i am a piece of air
i am a cloud
i am a bird
that can fly away
where there is no hurt

i am not here
i am not alive
i am a little girl
that nobody can see
because
she is only 4 years old
nobody can hear her
or stop the hurt
her head hurts
mommy
make her head not hurt
but
when she cries
it is only the scream
of
a little girl
that used to run and play
in her yard
she is a little girl
that one time
smiled and laughed
when her puppy kissed her on her nose
but
when those hands
touched the little girl
i think
the little girl
that someone once said was me
(died)
yes   that is what happened
she
just
died
and
can't come out to play today.

PERSONAL NURSERY RHYME
(Part One)

Twinkle twinkle tiny star
Way up in the sky so far
Daddy's coming! hurry! run and hide!
Her thoughts turn to patricide

Twinkle twinkle silent star
One more touch leaves one more scar
Daddy's coming! no, she can't tell!
Night becomes her private Hell

Twinkle twinkle child-life flame
Her young heart says she's to blame
Daddy's coming! can you hear her screams?
Vanished are her gentle dreams

Twinkle twinkle dimming light
Little girl so dreads the night
Daddy's coming! please hear her cry,
"Where do dreams go, God, when they die?"

PERSONAL NURSERY RHYME
(Part Two)

my little star has a pretty light
but i don't want to sleep tonight
a bad noise hurting in my head
monsters crawl beneath my bed

my little star has a silver light
in the sky it is shining bright
why can't jesus hear me cry
please give me wings and let me fly

my little star has a broken light
mommy and daddy always fight
it makes me scared but they don't care
i don't think that hurt is fair

my little star has lost its light
the *screaming* stole it from my sight
please little star come back to me
i need your light to help me breathe

UNDER THE STAIRS

"daddy's home!"
   big sister yells
             my heart pounds
      and
           dolly is tossed aside . . .
"The Bogeyman"
my head whispers
"The Bogeyman is home!"
          but
        before i can run
        he is beside me
      swinging me high above his head
          (guess it's just daddy today)
    he rubs my back
      (no daddy . . .)
      and says
"mommy said you were
bad again while I was gone"

               i look at her
                 but
          mommy says nothing

107

when daddy sets me down
i run downstairs
            and   hear his steps heavy in pursuit
                        thump   thump
                    thump   pause   thump
                        thump
            pause   thump   pause
    "go away
        i was a good girl . . ."
                        thump
                            thump
            but   The   Bogeyman
    isn't   even   looking
            for his bad little girl today

i hear him turn on the tv and yawn
            mommy yells "supper!"   so
    i know it is safe again
        he won't hurt me (it's just daddy, not The Bogeyman,
not The Bogeyman, not The Bogeyman, it's just daddy . .)
                    but i open the door
                    and look carefully to make sure
                        nobody can see me
and
        brushing the dust from my pants
                    i stand up
            and
            step out from my darkness
                        under the stairs.

FINDING THE CHILD

I walk into therapy
   head down
    (is there a sky today?)
       and
a bundle of
faded photographs
   (fading with time, just like me)
clutched tight in my hand
    ("pet it like your kitten, honey . . .
       yes, that feels very nice . . .")
I slump down in my chair
   (quiet, it's so quiet)
I give therapist my pictures
   (stupid, she doesn't care!)
      my face burns with shame
         and
I say to therapist
   "this is who I was"

                    I was
a kid on a bike
        (blue and white . . I have a scarred toenail)
playing in a sandbox
        (did I build sand castles?)
 a child on a porch
        ("don't slam that goddamn door again!")
 I was cute
        (did I wear pretty ribbons?)
I was precious
        (please . . please somebody love me)
I was just a little kid
        ("she sure knows a lot for her age!")
                    but
I don't know this person
        (has anybody seen me?)
I don't think she really existed
        (except in the darkness of my memory)
she has my face
        ("your sister is the pretty one . .")
                    yet
maybe it's not me at all
        (how could I forget the night she died?)
I can't remember her
        (blank, it's just all fuzzy and blank)
I was never a child
        (fly away, little one, fly far, far away!)
I wasn't here
        (under the stairs! look under the stairs, mommy!)

my head is pounding with pain

oh God
  I think
my father killed me
my father killed me
my father killed me   and
                I cried as I
                lay with my father
                      dying
                          but
              nobody came to help me

jerked back to reality
I look up at therapist
to see if she hears the child I can't find screaming . . .

                    she asks
                "are you okay?"
and
        all I can say is
            "why can't I remember being a virgin?"

ISOLATION

the sun rises
   right on time
           and
     I awaken from one more tortured night
          doing battle
          with old demons
         I needed to believe
           were already slain

the prison of silence
once again holds me captive
          and
        I say nothing

I go about my routine
          working
         staying busy
     so I don't have to think

I who claim healing
separate myself
from any who try to care
trivial problems
consume me
scramble my brain
and
pull   me
              in
                          different
      directions . . .

I isolate
because I am afraid
if I speak of my pain
I will once again
lose who I am.

MENTAL QUICKSAND

I step lower
    into the slate gray chasm
        of hopelessness that is
        water-logged sand covering my head
            and pouring into my lungs
    I begin to panic
    because I know
    once again
    I am trapped
    in mental quicksand

I feel the familiar
        slight change in texture
    a black hell of smooth consciousness
        luring me closer with unblinking seduction
            soaking through every gasping pore of my skin
            scraping metallic fingernails
            across the chalkboard of my sleep

                    it   methodically
            gleefully
                                    strangles me
and
        I choke with weak resignation
                knowing where I must go. . .

117

                                        I try to breathe
                                        but its putrid stench
                                        overpowers my senses
                            I try to move
                            but its ghost-hands
                            immobilize me
I try to believe
that there is one reason
I should fight this
    but in the end
    I take another step

                                                        down
            into this secluded world
            I am doomed to function in
                                and then
                    as I give in to the release
                    of convulsive hysteria
    I step back up to where I am real for one brief moment
                and understand fully
            that this is what it feels like
                to be buried alive.

QUESTIONS FOR MY MOTHER

mom
when I was born
did you
think that I was pretty
did you
call me 'cute' and 'precious'?
or
did you
lie in bed at night
feeling crushed
by yet one more burden
and
naming me as
one of your mistakes
wishing
you had never
given life to me?

mom
when
I took my first step
did you
clap your hands in delight
and
did you
run to get your camera
to preserve my special moment?
or
did you
sigh in your tired heart
knowing now
you'd have to watch me
more carefully?

was it
easy for you
to
turn away
and
think I was no big deal?

mom
when I started school
did you
hope and dream and wonder
what great discoveries
I might make?
or
did you
complain at the added expense
knowing it was
yet one more thing
you'd have to do without?
did you
dread what the teachers might say
about my bad behavior
and
then file it away
with everything else
that simply didn't merit
asking me about?

mom
when I was growing
into a young woman
why didn't you ask me
the reasons
for my hating to go to school?
when I told you
the boys were taunting me
why did you turn away?
how is it
that you never questioned
why I wore
one piece dresses to school
even when the snow was deep?
did it ever
cross your mind
that this might be a way
a 10 year old child
would try to keep away
hands that hurt?
why didn't you ask
why I ran from home
and
what made me so afraid?

was it that easy for you
to stay blind
to my pain?

mom
my life passed by
and now I am remembering . . .

        I asked so many times
        how it could be
        that everyone else I knew
        had memories of being a child
          and I had none

                you turned away
                    mom
              and I have to wonder
              how long have you known
                that my father hurt me?

   why
 do you choose
 to deny the truth?

        are you still afraid
        you might have to give up
        your material possessions?

were the nice houses
we lived in those years
worth pieces of my life?

mom
I'm finding the truth
I tried to tell you
and
you promised belief
yet when I told you
you turned away
once again
and so
I have made the journey
alone

mom
I need to know
one more thing
before I say good-by . . .

how can it be
that as a
little girl
I lay in my bed

night after night
weeping
and never once
did you hear
or

come to me
hold me close
comfort and reassure
me that you would
keep me safe?

mom
didn't you love me?

STANDARD ANSWER

pain
   locked tight within me
     can't escape
there is nowhere to go . . .

                  I own my pain
                    my rage
                    my silence
                    my terror
                    my wounded soul

I walk
 head down
  eyes lowered

            walls closing in around me
              I can't breathe!

I repeat the practiced lie
my standard answer
    when
     or if
anyone bothers to ask
how I am feeling

             I paste on a quick smile
               and say
              "I'm just fine"

I know the truth
I alone live it
                    as usual
          nobody seems to know the difference.

"FAVORITE"

last night
  in my dreams
I saw my childhood father
  standing above me grinning
     saying
over and over and over again
           "you're daddy's *favorite*!"

         I can't shake the dread I feel
           the gray skies outside
              match my mood

a thought flits across my mind
    and
  I reach for my dictionary
    know what I'm going to find
      what it's going to say
             and
         I am right . . .

"favorite"
according to Mr. Webster
means
"one unduly preferred"
or
"one favored above another"

oh God

oh God

oh God

I think
maybe it really means

"you weren't the only one"

MIRROR HANGING ON MY WALL

mirror hanging on my wall,
who's the most screwed up of all?
surely it's not plain old me?
my wounds scream for all to see!

mirror hanging on my wall,
I stand frightened by your call
wrinkles, scars, blank memory
surely you are kidding me!

mirror hanging on my wall,
I won't look at you at all!
dad molested me real good
his tribute to great fatherhood!

mirror hanging on my wall,
he beckoned and I heard his call
I went flying far away
HAPPY "END OF CHILDHOOD" DAY!

mirror hanging on my wall,
I want to kill him, once, for all
gouge his eyes, cut off his head
it feels *right* to wish him dead!

IN THE NAME OF MY FATHER

in the name of my father
                    I was
          molested   labeled   abandoned
                              and frightened
I lost
          my childhood   my dignity   my innocence
                              and my freedom . . .

in the name of my father
                    I felt
          ashamed   guilty   humiliated
                              and suicidal
I learned
                hatred   prejudice   distrust
                              and silence . . .

in the name of my father
                    I began
          running   escaping   hiding
                              and searching
I knew
                desperation   need   hunger
                              and sorrow . . .

                in the name of my father
                    I had
                    no friends
                    no family
                    no emotions
                    and
                    no God . . .

131

decades of time
lost

questions asked
of those who claimed to care
were denied
or went unanswered . . .

my spiral of destruction continued
unresolved
and unnoticed
but
I came to know
that the truth
is never wrong
and
in spite of
the names of my father's damage
I honor my grief
give name to my rage
and try to believe
that someday
I am going to heal
and join
the celebration
called
Life.

"DON'T TELL"

"don't tell . . ."
  "daddy loves you"
    "you're my favorite"
      "I won't hurt you" . . .
                    . . . so began the lies . . .

"don't tell . . ."
  "nobody will believe you"
    "everyone knows
      you play pretend" . . .
                    . . . so began the doubts . . .

"don't tell . . ."
  "your mother doesn't love you"
    "this is our special secret"
      "it would kill your mother" . . .
                    . . . so began the silence . . .

"don't tell . . ."
  "and I'll buy you
    a present"
      "if you behave
        I'll take you home soon" . . .
                    . . . so began the bribery . . .

"don't tell . . ."
  "stop your blubbering"
    "if you don't shut up
     I'll lock you in the car alone" . . .
               . . . so began the fear . . .

"don't tell . . ."
  "stupid little bitch" "bad girl"
    "you're just like your mother"
     "liar" "you're not special" . . .
               . . . so began the labels . . .

"don't tell . . ."
  "you can't go home"
    "nobody wants you"
     "you are a wicked, evil child" . . .
               . . . so began the hatred . . .

daddy
held secure in his hands
the dull-bladed hatchet of abuse

I alone bear the scars
from each blow he delivered
he hacked away
one touch at a time
until nothing was left
except a lifetime of
addictions   confusion   terror
and self-loathing

I called him
Daddy
      but his true names are
                  "Child-Soul Killer"
                 "Play-time Murderer"
                        and
                 "Daughter-Toucher"

                  yes
          he crossed the fine line
              that separates
                love
                     and
            hate

I don't want him dead

                   I want to know he lives each day
               staring at his own reflection
            looking at the mirror
                and
        seeing the maggots of his darkness
        crawling out of his soul
           to be a reminder of what he did
           to destroy an innocent child

he doesn't scare me anymore
        I am getting stronger each day
       as I emerge from the fog
       of long-buried memories . . .

sometimes
the ghost of his image
comes visiting
                    I hear it whisper
                    "hey, little girl
                            don't tell
                                    don't tell"
and
            when I hear those words
                                    I take a deep breath
                                    hold my head high
                    and
                    scream back my answer
            "YOU KNOW WHAT, DADDY?
            I TOLD ANYWAY!"

LEGACY

you had

warm food to eat

a place to live

money to spend

friends to talk to

God to pray to

cars to drive

laughter to enjoy

work to keep you busy

clothes to wear

women on the side

a wife at home

kids

freedom

and
you had
choices

                    then
one day you woke up
                                        thought about it
                    plotted out the details
        schemed carefully to get me alone
                                                    you
                                                decided

        you scared me into submission
                        you made me think it was okay
you
    chose
                    and
                        then you touched me

you
        told me
            to forget

                        you
                    were relieved
                    when I didn't tell

you
got real brave
  when nobody noticed

                            you
                        did not touch me
                    when it was not convenient
                and

you
    went on
            living your life
                leaving behind
                    your legacy of pain

it was I
who lay awake
all those nights
alone
afraid
silent
dreading
and always
wondering
if
you were going to walk
through my bedroom door

I can't say the words
"I hate you"
because I don't hate you
I hate myself
and
maybe it was my fault
just like you said

                              I lie here with the memories
                              trying to figure out
                              why you chose me
                                                   and
                              not someone else

I think about
how nice it would be
to believe
the pain will end
but
I can't believe that
                    because
                              I
                         haven't
                    believed
                              anything
                         for
                         years
                                        and
    yet   all my lifetimes later
          I am lying here with the truth
                    wishing again
                         I could be dead

I am alone with you

you are inside my soul

I want to kill you
    by
killing myself
        and
                nobody on the outside
even knows or cares . . .

I am alone with you
and
I am dying.

death

sometimes i lay awake at night
        and think about death . . .

        if death came to get me tonight
i would wear golden wings
        and fly with the angels
i would play hide and go seek on the clouds
        and not get tired
i would ask jesus to hold my hand
        and walk through the flowers in his garden
            and
i would sing a pretty song with all the other children
        about being safe and warm . . .

if death came to get me tonight
i would play hopscotch across
all the shining stars in heaven
i would say i love you every day
and nobody would call me little liar
i would use my big pencils to write a poem
about ballerinas dancing in the sky
and
i would never have to be afraid to close my eyes
and dream . . .

if death came to get me tonight
the hurt that lives in my heart
          would be gone forever
nobody would slap my face
          and call me bad stupid ugly child
god would give me toys to play with
          that nobody could take away from me
                              and
i would always be happy
          and cry no more tears at night
          on my little pillow . . .

sometimes
i feel very sad inside
and
sometimes
i feel very tired in my head
but
sometimes
i smile to myself
because
i think
death
might be a nice friend for me . . .

yes
sometimes i lay awake at night
and think about death.

THE MANY FACES OF DADDY

<u>WORK DADDY</u>
put in long, exhausting hours
smiled his winning salesman's smile
conversed easily with his clients
and
left behind echoing compliments
like
"he is so friendly"
"doesn't know a stranger"
"sure works hard"
his office a monument of achievement
trophies on his desk declare him
"SALESMAN OF THE YEAR!"

CHURCH DADDY
Sunday morning never absent
sharp in his best suit and tie
harmonizing perfectly, he
memorized every single word to
"The Old Rugged Cross"
underlined passages in his red Bible
(I know because years later
I found his beloved Holy Scripture Book
and looked at its dog-eared pages
just before I threw it in a trash can
and smoked a joint with my friends)
said "Amen" in all the right places
and on his way out the front door
shook hands with his good buddy the preacher
saying,
"wonderful sermon, Reverend Charlie, I learned so much"

FAMILY DADDY #1
paid the bills on time
drove a decent car
bought a nice house for the family
voted in the elections
took his kids to the circus
made sure we had good clothes
put presents under the Christmas tree
laughed at pranks and jokes
traveled with family on summer vacations
and
brought home a cute puppy or two

FAMILY DADDY #2
brooded silently in his office
for countless hours
yelled, "God damn it!"
when anyone made a simple mistake
argued with my mother
about sex at the dinner table
was unfailingly punctual
and
always seemed anxious
for Monday morning to come
so he could leave
for a week at work on the road again

DARK DADDY
took his kids camping
and
always managed to have me sleep next to him
put his hands between my small legs
at the drive-in movie
forced his hard penis into my mouth
in an isolated motel room
while he told me what a wonderful child I was
held my face upward
into the shower spray
when I started to cry
and
didn't give a shit
when I crawled out of his bed
cowering in a dark corner
listening to him snore
wishing
just wishing
I could die

I was a little kid
barely old enough to ride a bike
but I remember those hours
(shh! don't wake daddy!)
and someone please tell me
how can I forget
my raw, trembling fear?

yeah
the daddy of my childhood
had many faces
and I saw them all . . .

today
he smells like rotted garbage
　he is weak and feeble
　　(not so powerful now, are you, old man?)
　　　　　he spends his days
　　　　　　eating stale doughnuts
　　　　　　　　and
　　　　　　　　pissing bad coffee
he can't remember whom he told what
　he is distant to his children
　and humored by his wife
　　　　　he got busted
　　　　　by the IRS
　　　　　when they found out
　　　　　　he hadn't paid his taxes
　　　　　　　in almost 15 years
　　　　　　(proving there is no punishment
　　　　　　　for screwing your own child but
　　　　　　　not much tolerance if you try to
　　　　　　　screw the government)
his hands
　(God, I remember those hands)
　　　　are bent and crooked with arthritis
　　　and
　　　　　even simple tasks
　　　　　　confuse his senile mind

these days
I am beginning to stand a little taller
I am lifting my eyes off the floor
to see the world around me
instead of
counting tile dots
        I am learning to live
        rather than waiting to die
                            and
                                I sleep better at night
                                because now I know for sure
                                DARK DADDY
                                can't hurt me anymore . . .

the way I see it
is that
I know this is
one *very* big mess
but

just the same
maybe
living at peace within myself
will be
the best revenge of all.

MINE!

you sit across from me
talking about God
and how
He will take away my pain
you say
"He will never give you
more that you can bear"

                    you know nothing
                            about
                        how it feels
                    to see everything
                    I ever believed in
                        disappear into nothing
                        how it feels
                    to see lying at my feet
                        all of the lies
                            and
                        all of the secrecy
                        surrounding
                        what I used to call
                        "my family"

you know nothing
of what it was like
to be me
the little child
learning
adult survival games
wanting nothing
but to be loved
        and
finding instead
a life of
labels
  and
judgment
 that became
 the entirety of
    who I was
        and
 how my life would be

yes
I am
in a storm of emotion
I can't explain to you
without screaming
how delicious
the hate feels
toward those who hurt me
because
in your world
the blank world of
"GOD IS LOVE"
and
"JESUS SAVES"
your ears are deaf
your eyes are blind
and
pure soul-cleansing hatred
doesn't exist
and
you really
could never understand
if I told you
I don't need
or want God
to take my pain away
because
I earned the right
to feel it all . . .

maybe someday I will let go of my hatred
but right now
I own everything that I feel
and
not you
not God
not anyone else
can have it
because it is
MINE!

DON'T

don't talk to me
I can't hear you above the shrieking of my inner-turmoil
    don't advise me about feelings
        I want only to feel the sweet bliss of nothingness
don't try to fix me
my fragments will shred your mind
and make your soul bleed just as mine does
                don't look at me
                  I have no face or identity
        don't attempt foolish head games
        I wrote some of the rules
don't chase me
I've been running all my life
and know every escape route
            don't search for me
            I know how to become invisible
      don't try to read between the lines
      I'm not ever going to let you know me

don't touch me
    goddamn you
  don't you dare touch me
    my skin doesn't belong to me anymore
                        and
                don't tell me you love me
                don't say the words
            that are a lie I've heard all my life
don't try to get inside me
I know you are going to hurt me
and turn away from the pain that you see
                    so
    please
            please
                don't say you love me
                don't speak to me about comfort
                    when never once
                        have you taken the time to listen
                    to
            the weeping child within
                        that survived it all.

ONE PEBBLE

you stand behind
  your
    secure wall of accumulated knowledge
arms folded tightly
    across your chest
eyes narrowed and focused
    as if to dare me
    to answer the questions
    you slip nonchalantly
    into your thinly veiled attempt
    at casual conversation

                you believe you are so clever
                (and maybe once you were)
                        but
                what you still fail to notice
                is that I have grown
                and now I know you
                through eyes of experience
                given to me
                by the thousands that came
                before you

        I am not blind to the fact
              that
        you do not really see me
              at all

your mouth
   folds into the
      patronizing smile
      that time has taught you
      gets you the results you want
                  your lips
                   speak the
                cautiously-phrased words
             your pathetic brain believes
                   I want
                     or need
                     to hear
but
  every time I am near you
  my instincts are being fine-tuned

while
you were busy learning the rules
from a soul-less textbook
I was learning to survive
in a merciless world
created by someone just like you

so
before you get too comfortable in your belief
that you know how this story ends
remember
I wore Death's cloak
until it melted
to become my own skin
and
it never pays to fight
on the emotional turf of someone
who knows what it is like to die

foolish me!
in my naïve trust of you
I believed you were different!

all this time
you have continued to see
   what
         you want to see
         and that is your choice
I will never tell you
   how much you wounded me
      while hiding behind
      your masquerade of friendship
         or
         how tired I became
         fending off
      the pebbles of judgment
      you stupidly threw my way
                        so many times
                           you
                  nearly penetrated
                  the fractures in my soul
                  that still remained unmended
                        and
                  all that you pretended to be
                     threatened to reduce
                     what was left of my pain
                        to nothingness

               look into my eyes
                  if you can
                  and tell me
               would you even care?

no
you would move on after a while
from that which never got to be
justifying it somehow
as is your way
you would shake your head
in feigned disbelief
and ask "why?"
so you could live with yourself
(after all
that is what is expected of you)
but
you are not capable of caring
or comprehending
or accepting responsibility
for the damage you leave behind
and
no number of frantic apologies offered
or
sudden surges of sympathetic intelligence
can fix
what did not have to be broken
in the first place

someday
my friend
you will know the truth
of how much you hurt me
    but that pain has made me stronger
        than I think you counted on
            and
      the others who you believe
      are going to benefit
        from your disguises of
        "great humanitarian"
           and
        "public servant superstar"
           may not be as determined
              as I am
                  but
            before you bend down
              to pick up that one pebble of judgment
              that fits comfortably in your pale reality
      pause to remember my face
      if you've got the guts
                and
            let the truth of who I became
            be a reminder to you
            to walk carefully
            where you are not welcome

it is not wise
to throw stones
in the direction
of something
you cannot
and
will not ever
understand . . .

I am healing
and
I will survive you.

IN ALL FAIRNESS, GOD . . .

"Honor thy father
and
thy mother,"
so the Bible commands . . .

in all fairness,
God,
is there a commandment
telling fathers not to
molest their little children?

is there a commandment
telling mothers to
protect their babies
no matter what it takes?

I believe
honor is earned,
God,
and I can't
find it in my heart
today.

FORGIVENESS?

a
well-meaning friend
told me
that in order to grow
I need to forgive my father . . .

I
said nothing
but decided to
give it some
thought . . .

I
wonder
how can a person feel
forgiveness
toward someone
who won't even
acknowledge
the damage
he has done
let alone
apologize?

first
my father
made choices
that had nothing
to do
with caring about me
as a human being
let alone
his own flesh and blood
that God had entrusted
to keep safe

he
touched me
to satisfy his own selfish urges
he
used my mother
as an excuse
to dump his own
need to dominate and control
someone else
on my fragile mind

I guess
he figured
as long as he
bought nice houses
and
kept up the appearances
of 'normal'
(whatever *that* is)
while out in public
that it was okay
to treat me
and
everyone else at home
like shit

         my father
sat silent through the years
  while my life fell apart
                              he
                         saw the addictions
                         that began when
                         I was just 13

         he
    drove the car
when the courts sent me away
  (I was *incorrigible*, you see)
                         so yeah
                  I guess he must have thought
                     he was really
                         some great dad . . .

176

years later
he saw my destruction continuing
but was only concerned what everyone might *think*
when I
attempted suicide
at his house
I
continued losing
any shred of dignity I had left
but he
kept right on working
because
nothing mattered to him at all
except that
he
didn't have to acknowledge
any responsibility . . .

he grew old and senile
  got to forget
what he did to me
while I
not only survived
being molested
and used as his child-whore
but
now I have to survive
remembering it all again
  and
fix *his* damage

                              he stole my childhood
                                    but
                              now he gets more from me

              he
          has the sudden support
              of a family
            that hasn't
              cared about him for years
      he
keeps right on *stealing* from me
    and
          now someone tells me
            that
          I need to give him **more**
            by *forgiving* him?

                    it will never happen

            the only thing he will ever get from me
                      is my
                      hate.

JUSTIFIED

I have something
I need to say to you,
Mr. Child-Molesting Father,
so listen closely . . .

it has been
a source of confusion
that I can't
tap into the rage
I know I should feel
for all you did to me
perhaps it is because now
you are old and senile
but then I remember
you weren't that way at all
when you started
chopping my life
into tiny pieces

I can get angry with mother
for not protecting me
she knew what you were doing to me
and stayed with you
so she wouldn't be alone with 5 kids
she chooses now to blame me
but
that choice has nothing to do with me

I can feel hurt
by the stupidity of my sisters
who all these years
have had hardly anything to do with you
they won't explain *that*
but now come rushing forward
to try and present you
as
FATHER OF THE DECADE

it isn't hard at all
to be disgusted by brother
for shoving his hands down my pants
after you were finished with me
he took up where you left off
tell me
old man
he learned it somewhere
were you *his* teacher
in the art of
molestation and hate?
of course you were . . .
he has hated you for years

I can get mad
about being a little kid
with her first boyfriend
I loved him
and believed he loved me, too
he touched me the same way
you and brother did
I didn't fight him
why should I?
it was all I had ever known
from the men and boys
in my young life . . .
years later
it would be he
who called
and triggered the flood of memories
I sat with him a week later
still not remembering what he did to me
listening to his version
of what a wonderful childhood we had together
I believed him all over again
because I needed to believe something
had been right in my life
more time would pass before
the memory of his touching me would return
and it would be all I could do
to not walk up to his house
and drive
an ice pick through *his* evil heart

yeah
old man
it hasn't been too hard to get
real pissed off about everything else
but
then I found out
mother knew the truth
and didn't bother to tell me
I guess she was hoping
I wouldn't realize
the worst was yet to come

and it did . . .

I ask therapist
"why can't I get mad?"
she says
"don't worry
some of the memories are still fuzzy
and when the haze clears
all the pieces will be in place
anger will come when you
are ready to face it"

today
I was working on my journal
and decided to write down
what I knew about you
what I could remember clearly
and without conscious effort
I found the missing pieces
there was the truth
in black and white

I called therapist
said,
"I know what he did
I'm getting together enough money
to buy a plane ticket
go to where he lives
cut off his hands
gouge out his eyes
castrate him
and throw him bleeding
to the dogs"

I started crying my rage
screaming my pain
"I want him to suffer"
I whispered
"I want him to die" . . .

I talked with therapist
for a while
         good thing for you,
         Mr. Molester,
                  the only thing that is
                  keeping me off that plane
                  is knowing
         you are not worth going to jail for!
    so
instead of killing you
   (which is what you deserve)
I decided to make a list
of every reason I have to hate you
      it feels powerful
knowing I can hate safely
                  read my list
                  feel my pain
                  hear my rage
                        because
                  it is the last thing
                  you will ever get
                        from me
                        and today
                  I decided
                  you can't have my
                  life anymore . . .

186

209 REASONS WHY I HATE YOU
(not counting the ones I will remember later)

1. I hate you because you never loved me.

2. I hate you because you thought I would never remember what you did to me.

3. I hate you because you ignored me when I was a baby.

4. I hate you because you never told me bedtime stories.

5. I hate you because you convinced my mother to send me with you in the summer when you went away on business trips.

6. I hate you because you took me to motels on your business trips.

7. I hate you because you told everyone how special I was to you.

8. I hate you because you made me take showers with you at night after you had worked all day.

9. I hate you because you forced me touch your limp penis when we were in the dirty motel shower.

10. I hate you because you said it felt good.

11. I hate you because you had erections.

12. I hate you because you used my mother's lack of interest in you to justify touching me in ways you had no right to touch me.

13. I hate you because you made me sit on the motel bed and watch you masturbate.

14. I hate you because you took my tiny hands and made me touch your sticky semen.

15. I hate you because you turned off the light beside the bed.

16. I hate you because you said it was too hot to wear pajamas.

17. I hate you because you held me in your arms.

18. I hate you because you waited until I was asleep and then put your hands between my legs.

19. I hate you because you forced my legs apart.

20. I hate you because you said you were 'kissing' my private parts.

21. I hate you because you pinched me until I was bruised, then got mad when I told you that you were hurting me.

22. I hate you because you forced your penis into my mouth.

23. I hate you because you told me I was good for doing it.

24. I hate you because you scared me.

25. I hate you because I laid awake waiting for you to fall asleep.

26. I hate you because you snored.

27. I hate you for the times that you fell asleep and I crawled out of bed to sit in the dark corner of the motel room.

28. I hate you because you woke up.

29. I hate you because you got out of bed.

30. I hate you because you turned on the light.

31. I hate you because you picked me up and put me back in your bed.

32. I hate you because you told me that my mother did not love me and ignored me when I said I wanted to go home.

33. I hate you because you told me I was dreaming.

34. I hate you because you got up the next morning and acted as if nothing had happened.

35. I hate you because I was confused and cried.

36. I hate you because you left me in the motel room alone while you worked.

37. I hate you because you came back later in the day.

38. I hate you because you molested me again.

39. I hate you because you said I was bad.

40. I hate you because you looked angry when you talked to me.

41. I hate you because you told me over and over again how much of a burden I was to my mother.

42. I hate you because I started having a nightmare when I was 5 years old.

43. I hate you because I had the right to good dreams and what I dreamed about for years afterward was your penis in my face.

44. I hate you because I didn't understand the nightmare.

45. I hate you for the terrible, consuming fear of a little girl that was caused by that nightmare – that child wasn't someone else, you son-of-a-bitch, it was your own flesh and blood. It was me, daddy, it was me . . .

46. I hate you because unless you were touching me, you ignored me altogether.

47. I hate you because, when you took us kids on camping trips, you made me sleep with you under the pretense that it was because I was the youngest. That was a lie. You molested me again.

48. I hate you because you took my sisters and me to the drive-in theatre, and you let them sit on top of the station wagon while you put a blanket over your lap and forced me to touch you.

49. I hate you because you whispered how much you loved me.

50. I hate you because you reminded me repeatedly how I couldn't tell anyone our special secret.

51. I hate you because you told me nobody would believe me.

52. I hate you because I believed your words.

53. I hate you because you pretended nothing had happened when we went home.

54. I hate you, oh, how I hate you, because you smiled when you tucked me in at night.

55. I hate you because you walked into my room at night and scared me.

56. I hate you because I lay there wondering why my mother did not stop you from coming into my bedroom.

57. I hate you because you hid under my bed, reached in the darkness and touched me.

58. I hate you because when you left the room, I got out of bed and dressed myself.

59. I hate you because my child's mind thought wearing clothes to bed would stop you from touching me.

60. I hate you because the next morning, my mother yelled at me for coming to the breakfast table in wrinkled clothes.

61. I hate you because I didn't tell her why.

62. I hate you because I was terrified.

63. I hate you because I was so traumatized by what you were doing to me that I literally paralyzed my legs the summer I was 6 years old so that my mother would not make me go out of town with you again.

64. I hate you because I was unable to tell anyone what you were doing to me.

65. I hate you because you went to church.

66. I hate you because you were and still are a hypocrite.

67. I hate you because everyone thought you were such a wonderful family man.

68. I hate you because you were a liar.

69. I hate you because the way you treated my mother was wrong.

70. I hate you because the way you treated my brother was brutal.

71. I hate you because you ignored my sisters.

72. I hate you because you cheated on my mother.

73. I hate you because you were supposedly too busy to come to any of my school plays or functions.

74. I hate you because you were too busy to care about anything except satisfying your own selfish needs.

75. I hate you because you bought me presents to insure my silence.

76. I hate you because you thought your only responsibility was to make money and put food on the table.

77. I hate you because every time I was in the car alone with you, you told me how worthless my mother was.

78. I hate you because I felt alone.

79. I hate you because I was afraid.

80. I hate you because I was desperate for attention and even gave all my childhood toys away, hoping someone would like me.

81. I hate you because my mother told me I was a bad child.

82. I hate you because I believed her.

83. I hate you for the time we were flying kites out in the desert behind the house and you told me I couldn't do anything right just because the string got tangled.

84. I hate you because there were times in my childhood I sat in dark closets and under tables when you were home.

85. I hate you because nobody noticed.

86. I hate you because not once did anyone ask why I spent so much time playing alone.

87. I hate you for every time you picked me up and sat me on your lap.

88. I hate you because you took away any chance of my ever having any childhood friends that I could have told what you were doing to me.

89. I hate you because every childhood tear I ever cried never got wiped away.

90. I hate you because you ripped me off of a happy, normal childhood.

91. I hate you because I was your child and I deserved better than what I got from you.

.. moving forward in time ..

92. I hate you, Mr. Child-Molester, because I wore labels all of my life, and I did not deserve that.

93. I hate you because those labels are too numerous to mention.

94. I hate you because those labels hurt me every time I heard one.

95. I hate you because the years passed and I was molested at school by boys in my class.

96. I hate you because I thought nothing of being molested by the time it started.

97. I hate you because I was used to it.

98. I hate you because I didn't tell my teachers.

99. I hate you because I found out years later my teachers *knew* I was being molested at school and did nothing to stop it.

100. I hate you because the molestation plunged me deeper into childhood despair.

101. I hate you because when I should have been having fun I was simply enduring more molestation.

102. I hate you because my brother knew I was being molested.

103. I hate you because he used that knowledge to molest me himself.

104. I hate you because nobody stopped him.

105. I hate you because of the shame I felt about my changing young body.

106. I hate you for every minute of my self-hatred.

107. I hate you because I started using drugs when I was 12 years old and learned to escape the emotional pain by using.

108. I hate you because of my addictions.

109. I hate you for the first time I said "no" to sex and was raped.

110. I hate you because I was raped numerous times afterward.

111. I hate you because I felt that I was worthless trash.

112. I hate you because I was sexually promiscuous.

113. I hate you because I felt I was good for nothing but sex.

114. I hate you for the physical pain of miscarrying my baby when I was 13 years old.

115. I hate you because I suffered emotional losses.

116. I hate you because I could not tell my mother I was pregnant.

117. I hate you because I ran away from home dozens of times.

118. I hate you because not once did you come to see me in jail.

119. I hate you because my mother had to spend her days looking for me when I ran away from home.

120. I hate you for her pain.

121. I hate you because she worried.

122. I hate you because while you enjoyed warm meals, I scavenged for food out of a garbage dumpster.

123. I hate you because while you were warm and safe, I did whatever I had to do to have shelter.

124. I hate you because you pretended you didn't know it was your fault.

125. I hate you because you sent me away.

126. I hate you because you thought it would be better if I was somewhere else so you wouldn't have to deal with me.

127. I hate you because I was raped in jail by a trustee.

128. I hate you because nobody cared enough to know.

129. I hate you because while I was at the Children's Home, I was beaten so badly I had blood running down my legs.

130. I hate you because you paid Mr. Scales to keep me at the Children's Home.

131. I hate you because I came home and began running away again.

132. I hate you because you allowed the judge in Juvenile Court put me on Probation.

133. I hate you because I spent days in jail fighting off the sexual advances and comments of a bastard Probation Officer.

134. I hate you because he finally got me.

135. I hate you because you sent me away again.

136. I hate you because you never once wrote me a letter while I lived with Mr. Scales and his family.

137. I hate you because you and my mother started a fight with Mr. Scales at my high school graduation.

138. I hate you because that fight ruined my graduation.

139. I hate you because I couldn't have one single day that was special in my life without your ruining it somehow.

140. I hate you because you didn't stop the fight at our house the day before I married Ray.

141. I hate you because you sided with my brother.

142. I hate you because you said you wouldn't come to my wedding.

143. I hate you because you came anyway.

144. I hate you because I was unable to love a man.

145. I hate you because I learned from you how to 'endure' sex.

146. I hate you because I felt I could never be any different.

147. I hate you because you did not care when I gave birth to my daughter.

148. I hate you because you walked in the door right after she was born and didn't even look at her.

149. I hate you because you did not ask to hold her.

150. I hate you for molesting me when I was a child, you stupid worthless piece of shit, because when I had a child of my own, I was unable to nurture her.

151. I hate you because you stole my only chance at motherhood..

152. I hate you because you murdered my emotions.

153. I hate you because I knew I could not raise my child.

154. I hate you because I took her to live with her father.

155. I hate you because every time Ray cheated on me, I thought it was because I could not love him.

156. I hate you for my divorce.

157. I hate you because years later I continued trying to numb my pain by using drugs.

158. I hate you because I was beaten by the Police Officer several times.

159. I hate you because I found out later you knew he had beaten me and you did nothing about it.

160. I hate you because I got an abortion rather than risk getting more beatings by the Police Officer.

161. I hate you because I wanted to die.

162. I hate you because I felt it would be better to be dead than to keep hurting.

163. I hate you because I attempted suicide.

164. I hate you because I didn't even know why I hurt anymore.

165. I hate you because *nobody asked.*

166. I hate you because I decided to move to another state.

167. I hate you because my entire life was spent *running* because of what you did to me as a child.

168. I hate you because I married a second time.

169. I hate you because after all those years, I was still looking for someone who would love me.

170. I hate you because I was unable to love Steve.

171. I hate you because Steve hit me.

172. I hate you because he said I deserved to be beaten.

173. I hate you because I believed him.

174. I hate you for the first night I sought comfort and safety with a woman.

175. I hate you because I was unable to love women, either.

176. I hate you because I felt isolated.

177. I hate you because I *ran* again, searching, hoping I could find love and acceptance.

178. I hate you because I told my oldest sister that you had touched me.

179. I hate you because she did nothing to help me.

180. I hate you because not once did my telephone ring with a sister calling to see how I was doing.

181. I hate you for telling my mother she couldn't call me and for giving her a hard time about the phone bill.

182. I hate you for every time I needed support from a sister or from my mother and it was not there.

183. I hate you because I continued to increase my usage of drugs.

184. I hate you because I no longer cared about anything.

185. I hate you because I couldn't even cry anymore.

186. I hate you because I turned my pain inward.

187. I hate you for every night I was alone.

188. I hate you for every time I put a cut, burn or tatoo on my body.

. . and yes, there is more . .

189. I hate you because you blamed me for everything that was wrong in my life.

190. I hate you because I didn't know how to change the direction my life was going.

191. I hate you because I didn't bother to stop you.

192. I hate you for the life I never had because you molested me.

193. I hate you for the happiness I could not experience because you molested me.

194. I hate you because numbness was a part of my everyday existence, and because I didn't know how to be any different than what your abuse had made me.

195. I hate you because now I have to remember it all.

196. I hate you because of my family's denial.

197. I hate you because you are so senile you probably don't remember what you did to me.

198. I hate you because I know I wasn't the only one you molested.

199. I hate you because the others will remember, too, someday.

200. I hate you because you are at fault for the pain of my entire family.

201. I hate you because my family hates *me* for telling the truth about you.

202. I hate you because I can't have a family anymore.

203. I hate you because you have their belief all to your sorry self.

204. I hate you because I know I haven't yet remembered all you did to me.

205. I hate you because it is taking time out of my life now to repair your damage.

206. I hate you because anger is necessary to heal.

207. I hate you for every time I felt I deserved *nothing* from life.

208. I hate you because it never had to be this way and yet it was

and

209. I hate you because you are my father . . .

my wall of hate

I hate you I hate you I hate you I hate you I'm never going to forgive you you killed me you killed me I hate you I hate you I hate you you touched me you stole my soul you stole my mother you stole my life I hate you I hate you I wish I could kill you I hope you live forever I hope you die I want you to die like I did I hate you I hate you I hate you I hate you I hate you I hate you I hate you you stole my dreams you stole my light and I can't ever have it back I hate you I hate you I hate you I hate you and it hurts daddy you hurt me you hurt me and oh God please make it stop I hate you I hate you for making me remember I hate you I hate my mother for not believing me I hate you I hate you I hate you I hate myself I hate the pain I hate what you made me live through I hate you I hate you I hate you I hate you I hate you I hurt so bad why can't I die I want to die so it doesn't hurt anymore I hate you I hate you I hate you for all the pain it was your fault all of it I hate you I hate you I hate you I hope you suffer I hope you hurt I hope God kills you I hate you I hate you I hate you I hate you I hate you please please tell me why you hurt me please tell me it wasn't my fault daddy make the pain stop daddy I hurt so bad I want to die daddy why daddy please tell me why did you hurt me why did you laugh at me why did you hate me what did I do to make you laugh when I cried daddy please tell me I hate you and I loved you daddy was I bad did I do something to make you hurt me wasn't I good daddy I tried so hard to be your special girl daddy you said it wouldn't hurt but it did and you hurt me daddy why did you hurt me I'm so confused I loved you but you lied daddy you hurt me and I hate you I hate you I love you I hate you I hate you I hate you daddy you killed me daddy and I was just a little girl and you hurt me oh it hurts shit shit shit oh shit oh

205

I hate you, Mr. Child-Molester,
most of all
because
I get up every day
and
I know
somewhere
throughout the years of my life
you saw just how messed up things were for me
and
you had to know
somewhere in the back of your mind
I was suffering
because of
everything you did to me
but
never once
did you say to me
"I'm sorry". . .

yes
my hatred is strong
when you die
there will be joy
there will not one tear fall from my eyes
because
you are not a man
you are a monster
and
for every reason I find to hate you more
in the years yet to come
I will be completely
JUSTIFIED!

I KNOW WHO THE BOGEYMAN IS

3 a. m.

(scratch   scratch)
                        under my pillow
(movement)
                        beneath my bed

                                    I am 35 years old
                                    and
                                    The Bogeyman is back . . .

eyes clinched tight
paralyzed in childhood terror
    hand reaches from below
        (feather touch on my arm)
           whisper
        (shhh! I'm The Bogeyman!)
            invisible laughter
             white teeth
                (click click)
my bedroom door opens
  (Sleep Rule #1: never close the bedroom door at night!)
dim light in the hall
  (Sleep Rule #2: only the dark is safe!)
    reflects his shadow
    as he leaves
        (it's The Bogeyman, momma!
          The Bogeyman is in my room!)
   and
          then turns around
      to where I lie with the demons he left behind
         and
     reaches under the covers
      (remember The Bogeyman, Judy?)
     but when I open my eyes again
       he's not *there* anymore . . .

                                    yeah,
                                        tonight
                                The Bogeyman is back
                        and
I feel the child within
lift her weary head
                and scream into my brain
                "Daddy is The Bogeyman!"
                            as yet one more
                            memory veil falls away
        and
                I remember
that which I have carried
            deep within me for all this time
                            (little girl, I hear you)
            but never vocalized.

MY FATHER RAPED ME!

MY ANGER IS BLACK

my anger is black

it is in my face
   lips tightly closed, no expression
it is in my head
   pounding like a sledgehammer
it is in my shoulders
   muscles stretched taut
it is in my fists
   clinched in murderous longing
it is in my arms
   scarred from self-inflicted wounds
it is in my legs
   aching for release
      waiting for permission
         to walk the 1000 miles
      between where I rage
         and where the source of my rage
            lives with no remorse . . .

               my anger is black
   and it
      wears the face of my father.

VOICE

pain so crippling
    open wounds dripping

        people say
        "shut up!"
        "it doesn't matter"
        "I don't want to hear about it"
        and my personal favorites
        "you are *crazy*!"
        and
        "let the past be the past"

I say
"I'll shut up when I'm finished
talking about it
30 years I have been silent
I'm facing my past
so I can have a future"
and
"the child within my soul
needs to cry"

therapist talks about
finding
the child within

but
I was silenced so young
every part of me
went to sleep
and I did
the best that I could
because I had to survive

sometimes
I feel the child within
stirring around inside
        she has a voice

              man,
           she hurts so bad

no mother ever held her
sang her a lullaby

             no father ever loved her
          spent his time ignoring her
                 except
            when he touched her
             with hands of sin

I try to listen to the child
    make her feel secure
            she looks up
        from within me
        with tired, green eyes
                        so as
                            I feel her sighing
                                in my mind
                I take her hand
                        and
                            we go
                        for a walk
then
        sometimes . . .
                    sometimes . . .
                            I think
            I feel her trying to smile.

LULLABY FOR THE CHILD INSIDE

hush, little one, and please don't cry
my soul longs to sing you this lullaby
I'll give to you wishes while you sleep
now hush, little one, and slumber deep

I'll bring to you angels standing near
whose hands of peace will fade each fear
hush, little one, I'm here close by
now off to dreamland safely fly

I'll dream for you pixies on sparrows' wings
dancing on feathers while nature sings
I'll wish for you mermaids from the ocean sky
listen, little one, to the raindrops cry

I'll send to you meadows of flowers white
the sun to warm you with blissful light
I'll gift you with whispering winds that breathe
don't fear, little one, for I will never leave

hush, little one, and no tears cry
while I sing from my heart this tender lullaby
I feel the love sheltered in your innocent eyes
thank you, little one, for the strength to survive

217

LOST MOTHERHOOD

when I became a mother
I remember
holding my newborn daughter
in my arms
I remember
looking at her
waiting
for the
'rush of joy'
to come
like everyone said
would happen naturally

but it didn't . . .

I
tried to feel happy
I
put on the appearance
of a proud mother
but
at night
I would lie alone
with my fear
in my head
the demons haunted me
"why do I feel nothing inside?"
and
"why do I feel empty
in the place
where love and nurturing
are supposed to rest?"
but
there I had no answers

219

at home
I went through the mechanics
of 'good mothering'
I
bathed baby every day
fed her when she was hungry
and
put on my biggest smile
when people
looked at her
and remarked
how beautiful she was

holding baby
frightened me
I gave her toys
but did not know how to play
and
sometimes
when nobody was there to see
I would stand by her crib
looking at her sleep
weeping
for the love I could not give her

I
lived with my silent grief
and
blamed it on myself
figuring
it was one more thing
that was wrong with me

I tried to *feel*
but the emotions were
simply
not there

when
husband and I
divorced
the court gave me custody
but
it wasn't too long
before I knew
I was in
way over my head

I asked my own mother
"what is wrong with me?"
she got real mad
and said
"you are *not* a good mother"

but I knew that

I took my infant daughter
to live
with ex-husband and his new wife
they couldn't take care of her
so
his sister and brother-in-law adopted her
and
over the years
they have raised her
and made sure she was loved

looking back
at what I now know
about my own childhood
I realize
that
what fathers do to their daughters
sometimes
kills the part of them
that will
allow daughters to
nurture their own children someday
and
knowing this truth
causes sadness
in my heart
I'll never have another chance
to love my own child
and
the grief of lost motherhood
hurts
like nothing I have ever known . . .

my child
my child
if ever you read this
I want you to know
it wasn't your fault
that I couldn't raise you
I didn't know why
I felt so empty
but
it wasn't because
I didn't try to love you
I just didn't know how . . .

I'm sorry if I hurt you
so
please
please
don't hate me.

PART III

HEALING TRANSFORMATION

ROOM FOR A BUTTERFLY

this morning
I stepped outside
to breathe the cool spring air
and
greet the sunrise

                                      I stood quietly
                                        clearing my mind
                       listening to the birds
                       chattering impatiently
                       high in the trees
after a while   the neighborhood woke up   people drove by
           everyone in a hurry to get to work on time
and

       I turned to walk back inside
          when

            across my path of vision
          a yellow butterfly floated by

                              and

      I watched its tranquil flight
            on delicate wings
            riding the wind
                with nowhere important to go
           and
            I smiled . . .

all I have ever known
is how to cope and exist
but today
I made room for a butterfly
in my heart
and
I realized
I am learning how to live.

BREAKING HABITS

my hands start trembling
when I wrap a present
    I hear my father say
        "crease those edges!"
        "match that design!"
        "don't rip the paper!"
so I
    leave the edges loose on purpose
    use solid-colored paper
    repair a small rip with transparent tape
                    and I
                    feel good . . .

my chest starts to tighten
an hour before appointment time
    I hear my father say
        "never be late!"
        "people respect punctuality!"
        "always be at least 20 minutes early!"
so I
    make myself be 20 minutes late
    the receptionist smiles when I walk in
        and says
    "we'll be with you in a minute"
                    and I
                    feel wonderful . . .

I feel panic setting in
thumbing through my address file
an index card isn't in its proper place
       I hear my father saying
              "if you are organized
                you are a success"
so I
     dump all the cards out on the table
     pick them up and throw them in the air
                   and I
              double over laughing . . .

today
my package looked quite nice
my appointment didn't get canceled
I threw out all the index cards
and changed
over to an address *book*
so I
quit being prisoner
to my father's habits
at least for one day
and I am
powerful.

DEATH OF THE FAIRY TALE

the knife of truth
        plunges deeply
      into the core of my identity
               and with each thrust
         memories buried
         are exhumed
       from their childhood grave
        of abuse

in silent meditation
      I see the death
        of who I was

             and the rebirth
           of who I really am

I see the child
reaching for her mother
longing for recognition
        and
acceptance of her individuality
                I see her tears of confusion
                flowing tiny rivers down her cheeks
                when mother does not know enough
                to take one minute from her day
                to comfort and nurture this child
                whose life she helped create

I see the child
    a mere movement in the shadows
    feel her fear
          and
    know intimately the shame she feels
    at not understanding what she has
    done to make father hurt her
        one touch from his hands
           and
        her mind absorbs his power
        believes his words
          "mother doesn't love you"
                   and
             so begins her life-long search
             for just one person who will care

I see the child
running through fields
of non-existence
there is no joy
in her young life
                    so she runs from home
                    chased by haunting echoes
                    of savage laughter
                    and
disappears into a grown-up world
she is not prepared to confront

I see the child
thirsting for elusive compassion
hungry for safety
                    I feel her shiver as she seeks shelter
                        in caves of stone
                    rat-infested shacks of retreat
                            and
                    rusted car skeletons tossed aside

I see the child
beaten for reasons unimportant
she is growing up fast
                              and
                    defiant survival dictates
                  that she learn to play the game
                            called
          "Say What You Think They Want To Hear
           Or You're Gonna Get Beat Real Bad"

                         she has long ago accepted that
                         things won't ever be any different
                              in her world
                                  and
                       she bears the burden
                       of a perished soul
                              solitary and wise
                              beyond her time
                    her eyes are down-cast
                         as
failure and defeat become her only friends

sometimes she remembers
futile attempts at loving
emotionless motherhood
aching addictions
and
the days she was too tired to try

some
would call her strong
but mostly she is numb
anesthetized by dope and life
she can't cry anymore
because there is no reason to care

she is
woman-child
familiar with ears that do not hear
and eyes that do not see
she wonders about the thousands
who live in glass houses
of make-believe
unaware that she awaits for one soul
to stop and ask her
"what is your pain?"

her memories become
scattered fragments of conversation
and
faded photographs of a little girl
who wears her face
yet is a forgotten stranger

I was this child and am
  now a woman grown

                        catapulted out of the despair
                              in my darkest hour

memories recovered
      waves of confronted emotions
                        it wasn't too difficult
                        to create a safe Fairy Tale
                        to believe in

I believed
            finally
        father would apologize for my pain
        mother would hear the cries of her child
                        and there could be
                                unity
                                and
                                healing
                    in acceptance of truth

    but
the Fairy Tale
        died a long, slow death
            as I awoke to find
                the chaos of denial
                was the path of their choice
                        I struck out in my pain
                            honest anger
                        toward those
                        who claimed to love me
                                yet
                        would not acknowledge
                        my right to the truth . . .

I have spoken the eulogy for my past
    am no longer a victim
        but a survivor
            whose choice is for healing

                            what is past
                        cannot be changed

    what is dead
    must be buried

           there is sadness and grief
              for my losses
                    but I have no regrets
      for perhaps now
        I can learn to live.

CROSSROAD

I come to the place in my healing
                    the crossroad
            which separates
                            Looking Back
                            and
                            Moving On

the clouds of doubt
            break apart
                    sunlight filters in
                        and
                    a soft breeze
                        gently caresses my cheek
                            as
                            I become a woman
                                finding peace

the pain is released
    my wrath is vented
              and
the heavy burden
    of
        victimization
            is lifted from my shoulders

                I see my truth
              through the eyes
             of honest healing
                  and I can understand that
                      the torment and grief
                    of
              lost childhood remembered
             is part of who I am
                but no longer
            the entirety of
                my identity

I have slowly untangled
      the dark threads of my life
            that were woven by the choices
                        of my father
                              and now
                        I marvel at the opportunity
                        to weave a Life Tapestry
                              of my own

            from pastel shades
            of
                  experiences
attitudes   and healthy choices
            I choose a pattern
      unique   colorful   reflective of
                                    freedom from self-doubt
                                    and
                                          new life

it is my own
      and I delight in the creation
            of friendship and discovery . . .

as I stand at the crossroad
    viewing my options
                    I realize
              I have begun leaving behind
            what has always been familiar
and feel the flutter of anticipation
    as I explore
      what is
             Yet To Be

                 I am
     dreaming in the world around me
    dancing to the beat of my own song
      sitting silently in calm meditation
        and
 searching that which I have come to know
    to find my own suitable style

I pause
    for one last look back
    at the path on which I have journeyed
                        my head is held high
                    as I
            take a deep, cleansing breath
        and then I
hear the laughter
    of a child growing
        and   feel the words whispered
        "all is well with my soul."

AUTUMN CLOUDS

tonight
I stepped outside
to touch the cool autumn breeze
and
looked to Heaven
thanking God
for yet one more day of life
then
I smiled in my solitude
when the storm clouds parted
and
for one brief moment I saw
an angel
floating wistfully across the moon.

ERASING OLD TAPES

I've been feeling
really good lately
upbeat
positive
energetic
and
excited about the changes
taking place
where they count the most

then today
one of my
lifelong old enemies
paid a repeat visit
INSECURITY
tiptoed right up behind me
started playing old tapes
recorded in the voices
of those from my past
it isn't as loud as
it has been usually
but
the message is still
very clear

the haunting voice
called
INSECURITY says
"you can't do it!"
"your past is going to get you!"
"you look like crap!"
"you'll never be able to afford anything!"
"nobody really likes you!"
"you are not important!"
"you have such a long way to go!"
"you can't do *anything* right!"
"you have no talent!"
"you are useless!"
"you have nothing worth talking about!"
"you are fat!"
and then
I hear my mother's voice
chiming in
to say
"just another failure to put on your list,
right, Judy?"

I shake my head
to clear it
make some *new* tapes
recorded in my *own* voice
I say
"I've done it!"
"the past is buried and
can no longer control me"
"I give myself permission
to buy myself something pretty!"
"I have a savings account!"
"I made a difference
when I listened to the pain
of a friend today"
"look at how far I've come on my journey!"
"people care about me –
and I'm letting them!"
"I'm writing a book
that someday will help others"
"I'm comfortable in my own skin"
and
in response
to my mother's contribution
and comments
about being a failure
I celebrate
that my feet are
on a path to healing
then I smile
and
think to myself
"I'm getting rid of the garbage"

I have to laugh about this
because
I know I'm getting stronger
my life has been spent
looking at the dark cloud
(you know, the one that followed me everywhere)
and
waiting for the proverbial ax to fall
(you know, the one swinging above my head)

now
it only happens *sometimes*
and
the coolest thing of all
is that when
INSECURITY
comes knocking at my door
and wants to rain on my parade
I know right away
what face it wears
and
playing my own new tapes
a little louder
I
win one more battle
and
smile when I say,
"you are not welcome here anymore!"

ON DISCOVERING FLESH

I look at my feet
callused and caked with dirt
I walk barefoot most of the time
because
it feels good
for my feet to touch the sun-kissed earth
I think about
the weight they have carried
and
the thousands of miles they must have walked
and
I thank God
for my tired, wide feet

> I look at my hands and arms
> weep for the scars of past self-hate
> I flex each finger
> thinking about all that they have
> held in their grasp
> the stories they could tell
> and
> I thank God
> for feelings of acceptance
> and new self-respect

I look at my flesh
touch it all one inch at a time
marvel with a grin on my face
at the
stretch marks
wrinkles
and
different textures . . .

I think about
what this flesh of mine has survived
and
where it will be with me in the future
I smile
and
then start laughing
because
I have just delighted
in being
plain old
me!

HEALING TOUCH

twelve letters
    placed systematically   and
        strategically
    one after the other
      to
formulate two words
    that when given as a gift
        from one broken soul to another
          are both
        the definition
    and
        the solution
        to
      the most basic need
      of all humanity . . .

    my skin
    aches
for the solace
    of
healing touch.

A SINGLE ROSE

this a time of peace
in my life
there is
reflection
of the journey
I have traveled
these past months
and
a time
of soul rest

the darkness of night
is no longer a threat
but a safe retreat
the night sounds of silence
welcome my dreams
and
it is then
that I can truly
appreciate
all that is
good in my life

I do not practice
organized religion
but have discovered
spiritual cleansing
in
acknowledgment
of a Deity
much greater than I
as I walk this earth

I am aware
that throughout my life
there were times
I should not have
survived
but did
and looking back
at the years of
destruction
and
devastation
which was my existence
I marvel
at a Power
that kept me safe
against all odds

it feels good
to have found faith to believe
there is more to life
than merely existing

I swore in my time of anger
there would be no forgiveness
for my father
I could not understand his choices
or
his refusal to acknowledge
but
putting that aside
I let go of the anger
and
somewhere along
the path to my own healing
feelings of pity
and compassion
toward all who hurt me
replaced the rage
and
it feels good
not to hate

perhaps someday
forgiveness will come
but
for now
forgiving myself
has been hard enough
and
honesty
about what I feel
is
what is most important

last night
I dreamed of a living garden
it was not filled with flowers
but the faces
of people who have
stood beside me
through my healing
offering
unconditional love
belief
support
respect
and
encouragement

I awoke
feeling inner-calm
and
thinking about
what it might mean

as I sat in
quiet meditation
the thought came to mind
"God's world is a blossoming garden
and in His bouquet
we are each a
single
fragrant
rose" . . .

it is awesome
to dream the dreams
of the healing.

GARAGE SALE RABBIT

driving down the street
enjoying the bright summer day
I see a neon sign
in a yard
"Garage Sale Today"
it says
so
I stop in to browse

there are
boxes of old books
(not interested)
long rows of tools
(boring)
assorted glassware
(got all I need)
and
two over-priced chairs
(yawn)

the gray-haired lady
whose stuff it is
says
"looking for anything special?"
I answer politely
"not really"
and
continue on

the gray-haired lady likes to talk . . .

"damn hot out today
gonna be glad when it cools off some"
she mutters
I nod in agreement
and encouraged
she says
"I got some crafts and such
back in the garage
hand-made dolls, too,
if you wanna see 'em
dolls is
kind of a hobby of mine
but
I don't do it much anymore
I guess what kids want nowadays
is
dolls that pee and talk"

I laugh
and
following her lead
I make my way back *very* casually
(because I am, after all,
The Adult Who Has No Time For Nonsense)

sitting
on an old washing machine
that has surely known better days
I see
big dolls
with frilly dresses
little dolls
with plastic eyes
dolls by the dozen
every
shape
size
and
color

I turn to leave
when
out of the corner of my eye
I see a
pink ribbon
poking out of the pile

I'm curious
so I
move to look closer . . .

she is
a white rabbit doll
with a smudge of dirt on her ear
she wears
five rosebud ribbons
a maroon-colored blouse
and
pink ribbon slippers

my heart skips a beat
when I pick her up
she's
a ballerina rabbit
and
around her waist
is tied
a white lace tutu

I stand in the corner
of a dirty garage
holding
a white garage-sale rabbit
close to my heart
as
I hear a memory
from the distant past
a child's happy voice
saying
"when *I* grow up
I'm gonna be a ballerina!"

a tear
rolls down my cheek
because
I know
whose voice it is . . .

a few minutes later
Sissy
The Ballerina Rabbit
with
her embroidered smile
and
black button eyes
sits contently
in her ribbons and lace tutu
safe in my heart
and
on my living room couch . . .

she is my gift today
to the child
who lost
her ballerina dreams
long, long ago.

I REMEMBER A LITTLE GIRL SMILING

when I need safety
and
a place to rest
when the walls
seem to be closing in
from having to confront my past
I bow my head
and give thanks to God
for memories that I can recall
of
a little girl that smiled . . .

I remember
a yellow Slip and Slide
stretched across the yard
my favorite store – Ben Franklin
Mrs. Williams, my third grade teacher
and
glasses of ice cold lemonade

I remember
mud pies lined up on the front wall
horned toads with soft tummies
hiking with my sisters
and
a parade with a Bullwinkle balloon

I remember
Gulliver's Travels at the walk-in movie
a Slinky in slow-motion creeping down the stairs
a white mouse named Howie
and
chasing geese through sprinkler rain

I remember
Christmas lights that lit the city
square cinnamon suckers that were 2 for 5 cents
Captain Kangaroo and Mr. Green Jeans
and
a chimpanzee named Susie Spit at the zoo

I remember
corned beef with honey glaze for Sunday dinner
trick-or-treating when it was safe
walking to school with a kid named Kelly
and
an Easy Bake Oven that I loved

I remember
walking in the warm summer rain
taking apart an Etch-a-Sketch to see the silver stuff
riding on a roller-coaster at the State Fair
and
a kaleidoscope that kept me in awe

I remember
playing with a paddle ball
Buster Brown and Twiggy Shoes
Tinkerbell on "The Wonderful World Of Disney"
and
throwing up all over a
coconut-covered birthday cake

I remember
Cooties, Mousetrap, and Hopscotch
finding out there was no Santa Claus
getting my big toe caught in
the spokes of my blue bike
and
every single word to the "Hokey Pokey"

I remember
my Shetland pony named Amy
a Dachshund named Herman
a red fox cub named Ferdie
and
a Siamese cat named Gomer

I remember
brother falling through the plaster
of a garage ceiling
sister using Nair to thin her eyebrows
mother being in a car wreck
and
running into the house for a dime
when the Ice Cream truck came around

it may not seem like much
to anyone on the outside
but
for quite some time
all the memories surfacing
were of
abuse and pain
I couldn't remember
any childhood happiness
and
it hurt
to feel the sadness
of a child so alone

remembering happy events in my childhood
doesn't erase my father's choices
or
how my life was because of them
but
some of the blank spaces
are now filled in with laughter
and
there is a sense of satisfaction
that
I have one more chance
to
laugh and play again
so
no matter what else happens
I will treasure always
this joy
of remembering in my heart
the face
of a little girl
when she smiled.

PEEK-A-BOO!

the fog murmurs gently
   as it folds neatly in around me
      coiling damp fingers against my flesh
    trembling with opaque insistence
      and
    concealing all that I desire to see

          then
        just when
      I have given up all hope
     of glimpsing anything but
          smoke-gray skies above me
  the fog sneaks away on wee tiptoes
           as quietly as it came today

                I look up
                        to see the clouds break apart
                                and paint themselves across the heavens
        and
                a spontaneous smile
                        plays at the corners of my lips
                                when I hear the voice
                                        of the happy child within me
                                squealing
                                        "Peek-A-Boo, Mr. Sunshine!
                                        I see you!"

this morning
I slow-danced
in the healing embrace
of
another beautiful day.

ON THE OTHER SIDE OF THE SCARS

on the other side of the scars
        winter ice becomes spring blossoms
        raging rivers become tranquil waterfalls
        storm clouds become blazing sunsets
        and
        moonless nights become golden dawns . . .

on the other side of the scars
        ruthless judgment becomes forgiving compassion
        dark foreboding becomes breathless anticipation
        pungent bitterness becomes enticing fragrance
        and
        past suspicion becomes innocent trust . . .

on the other side of the scars
      weary searching becomes blessed surrender
      hungry need becomes gentle sharing
      savage grief becomes radiant laughter
          and
    midnight weeping becomes inexhaustible joy . . .

on the other side of the scars
      endless confusion becomes peaceful enlightenment
      mute existence becomes poetic expression
      childhood trauma becomes mature wisdom
          and
    hostile chaos becomes unwavering faith . . .

on the other side of the scars
the paralyzed damage
of my frightened tragedy
is now transformed
into the anchored strength
of
healing grace
and
I am emerging.

PROGRESSIVE DEFINITION

Love
is
the ultimate quenching
of
mutual need
that binds all other emotions
together
as one
perfect expression.

CHOICES

Today I choose to be happy

I will visit with a neighbor who is suffering,
I will take time from my day to smile at a stranger,
and
I will reach out a hand of friendship
to someone who might feel alone . . .

Today I choose gracious living

I will accept my defeats as well as my victories with style,
I will replace negative thoughts with positive affirmations,
and
I will open my mind to changing directions . . .

Today I choose spiritual healing

I will humbly ask my God to guide my life-path,
I will be patient with others
even when I cannot understand their choices,
and
I will pray for a forgiving heart
toward those who have hurt me . . .

Today I choose new attitudes

I will quiet my own inner-chaos long enough
to hear another person's point of view,
I will take the risk to say "I love you" to someone
who may not seem lovable,
and
I will become stronger, even though I realize
that to feel this new strength I may be required
to suffer more necessary pain . . .

at the beginning of this day
as
the moon sighs her last breath
and
the sun bursts through the storm clouds
I will
bow my head in meek gratitude
for all that God
has given me
and
I will grow . . .
and I will grow . . .
and I will grow.

I WEEP FOR THE CHILDREN

I weep for the children
whose empty eyes stare
at those who can't see them
and won't stop to care

I weep for the children
who know not to speak
their world is cold silence
as warm love they seek

I weep for the children
who no longer cry
so quiet in their hunger
their gentle souls die

I weep for the children
who suffer the blame
for choices made against them
they exist in the shame

I weep for the children
whose wounds never heal
they cope with the anger
but no longer feel

I weep for the children
I weep for lost time
I weep for their darkness
for once it was mine

IT SHOULDN'T HURT TO BE A CHILD

dreams from cotton candy spun
carousels on wishes run
laughter filled with magic fun –
it shouldn't hurt to be a child

meadows frolic, flowers grow
angels shadow virgin snow
birthday cakes with candles glow –
it shouldn't hurt to be a child

toes that wiggle in the sand
ladybugs rest safe in hand
God has whispered the land,
"It shouldn't hurt to be a child"

flying in a tire swing
prayers take flight on fairy wings
roses to the dewdrops cling –
it shouldn't hurt to be a child

stars that twinkle in the night
tender breezes bathed in light
lullabies that calm all fright –
it shouldn't hurt to be a child

"now I lay my soul to sleeping
I ask you, God, to quiet my weeping
to Your promise of peace I'm keeping –
sometimes it hurts, God, to be a child"

CONTINUING THE JOURNEY . . .

I am constantly amazed at the changes that have taken place in my life from the start of my healing journey until the time I completed compiling my work to share with others in this volume of poetry. Whenever I hear, "Time and truth heals," I smile because I have experienced this firsthand.

Slowly and tentatively, I have emerged from the darkness and pain of remembering the details of my abuse that once consumed my every waking hour. I know that in the years to come there will be much more about my past that I will discover, yet I am secure in the knowledge that God is with me as I continue to move forward in the beautiful sunlight of living life to its fullest. The nightmares that haunted my sleep for years have ceased. The black shadows of my past have vanished, and I feel as if I have stepped into a vibrant neon world. I am thrilled to be enveloped in the sights, sounds and textures of new life stirring within my soul; I have escaped from a living death and feel reborn. I no longer view this rebirth of life through the clouded vision of a victim but through eyes that have been cleansed by the chosen pain of seeking my truth; I am proud to be a survivor.

Throughout the past five years I have learned much about the resilience of the human spirit and its ability to be completely regenerated through an honest confrontation of each fear. It saddens me that we live in a world that has become callused to hearing about violence against innocent children and now turns a deaf ear to children's cries for help. Survivors must continue to break the silence surrounding all forms of abuse and violence, giving voice to their individual truths before decades are needlessly lost from the lives of children everywhere. Ideally, our world will someday be a safe place for children to play, grow, and learn without fear. Until then, each survivor can only tell his or her story without apology and trust God to open the minds, hearts, and ears of those who most need to hear it.

My prayer for those of you who have shared my journey through reading The Invisible Child is that you will love one another and look for the good that rests inside all mankind. Each of us, no matter the age, race, sexual orientation, or social status, has experienced the pain of emotional wounds and the fracture of spirit on some level; I am sorry for your pain, my friends, and I am sorry if at any time in your life you have felt alone and afraid with pain that was not given voice or acknowledgment. Reaching out a hand of compassion, forgiveness and love – even when we can't understand the choices others make that hurt us – will move mountains. Imagine, if you can, one moment in time, when, instead of being imprisoned in the darkness of hate, we each took one step forward in the light of spiritual love and allowed this to be the common thread that could bind our hearts, souls and minds together.

Our world would forever be transformed.

Though I would not wish what I survived upon anyone, my life is coming full-circle and I know I wouldn't be who I am had my life been any different. I am humbled to have been given the opportunity to help others through my voice and my writing, and anticipate with great joy the growth that still awaits my discovery as I continue my future journey. Though the blessings that encompass my life are countless, the best reward of all is being able to reflect on the path my truth has allowed me to travel thus far, and in the quiet of night to hear the giggling voice of the precious child who survived the horror – and the healing- whisper in my soul, "I'm glad I was born."

God bless
and
keep safe
the invisible child.

Judith Ann Lee

December 1998

Email:
healingheart @ Vtechworld . com

You may contact the author regarding public speaking
engagements or to share personal comments about
<u>The Invisible Child</u> by

E-mail: ~~**heartwhispers2@webtv.net**~~
~~or~~
~~FAX: (512) 853-5630~~

Author WebSite address:

http://invisiblechild.tsx.org

(Sorry, no book orders by FAX or E-mail)

297